The Christian *and the* Sword

The Christian and the Sword

AN ANABAPTIST MANIFESTO OF 1577

PETER WALPOT

Preface by Art Wiser

Introduction by Leonard Gross

Translated by Elizabeth Bender and Emmy Barth Maendel

PLOUGH PUBLISHING HOUSE

Published by Plough Publishing House
Walden, New York
Robertsbridge, England
Elsmore, Australia
www.plough.com

Plough produces books, a quarterly magazine, and Plough.com to encourage people and help them put their faith into action. We believe Jesus can transform the world and that his teachings and example apply to all aspects of life. At the same time, we seek common ground with all people regardless of their creed.

Plough is the publishing house of the Bruderhof, an international community of families and singles seeking to follow Jesus together. Members of the Bruderhof are committed to a way of radical discipleship in the spirit of the Sermon on the Mount. Inspired by the first church in Jerusalem (Acts 2 and 4), they renounce private property and share everything in common in a life of nonviolence, justice, and service to neighbors near and far. To learn more about the Bruderhof's faith, history, and daily life, see Bruderhof.com. (Views expressed by Plough authors are their own and do not necessarily reflect the position of the Bruderhof.)

ISBN 978-0-87486-879-1 (2nd Edition)

This translation originally published in the January 2009 issue of the *Mennonite Quarterly Review* as "Concerning the Sword: A Hutterian Apologia of 1577." Used with permission. Front cover art: Jan Luyken, *Louwerens Janss Noodtdruft, of Delft, A.D. 1577.*

CONTENTS

Preface *vii*

Introduction *xi*

Nonviolence in the Old Testament 1

Nonviolence in the Gospels 14

The Apostles on Nonviolence 35

Arguments of the World 52

Further Considerations 78

Notes *95*

PREFACE

THE *CHRISTIAN AND THE SWORD* is the fourth article of the *Article Book,* a major doctrinal statement of the Hutterites of the sixteenth century. Its author is not named but was probably the Hutterian bishop Peter Walpot (1521–1578). The book deals with beliefs and practices of the Hutterites in regards to five significant topics: baptism of adults, the Lord's Supper, community of goods, conscientious objection to military service, and marriage between believers and unbelievers.

The book is not a theological tract, but rather, like other Anabaptist writings, a collection of biblical texts topically arranged to prove the position of the church with regard to the question at issue. The original title of the larger volume, *A Beautiful and Pleasant Little Book Concerning the Main Articles of our Faith,* is quite colorless; more to the point is the title used in the *Chronicle of the Hutterian Brethren: The Five Articles of the Greatest Conflict Between Us and the World.* It does not contain a complete system of Anabaptist thought but only a collection of those points and arguments that distinguish them and justify their particular stand.

A 1610 codex of this *Article Book* is one of the treasures that Eberhard Arnold, founder of the Bruderhof, was given as a gift by his Hutterian hosts in North America during a year-long journey to them in 1930. It is carefully crafted, with the name "Darius Heyn" written in the front (a minister in the Hutterian Church from 1599 to 1618). Arnold called this book: "One of the most valuable gifts of my whole American journey for our Bruderhof." (It is preserved in the Bruderhof Historical Archive in Walden, New York (catalog number EAH 227).

How highly he prized this codex is shown by the fact that he located another copy – handwritten around 1797 – and, in spite of serious eye trouble, spent weeks comparing the two. Wherever some page or word or letter was missing or illegible in the copy he was given, because of damage over the centuries, he wrote detailed instructions on how corrections should be made. Arnold's thorough description of the codex and his instructions take up twenty-four pages. This work is a wonderful testimony to his scholarship and his excitement about the early Hutterian manuscripts. He wrote in his description of the codex:

> [The fourth article] comprises 107 points. The first twenty-five, ranging from the time of Noah through that of the Israelite kings to the testimony of all the prophets, including Esdras, illustrate the meaning of government with its use of violence, on the one hand, and of the nonviolent kingdom of Christ on the other. Of special significance is point 5 with the parable of the trees (Judges 9) which would have to give up their oil, their sweetness, and their wine in order to rise

to power, with the result that the thorn bush comes to hold sway. Points 26 through 52 show how Jesus in the Gospels will not let those who are his have any part whatever in bloody violence or in executive or judiciary power, even though Jesus also acknowledges that government is necessary in the world. The following points, 53 through 69, prove from Acts, the apostolic letters, and Revelation that the apostles did not allow Christians to be rulers, that is, to return evil for evil, but that they recognized the ruling powers. These points also define the limits within which the apostles acknowledged governmental power, as well as the offices and weapons they assigned to Christians, and how their love and the governmental sword are opposed to each other. Point 69 throws a light on the time when this document was drawn up by stating: "Whenever they can find a single true Christian who leads only two or three people out of their ungodly lives and their adulterated church, such a person they put to death thirstily, and cannot tolerate him." And at the end of point 68: ". . . who even today put the members of Christ into prison and kill them because of their faith."

Point 70 once again throws a clear light on the distinction between Christ and the world with respect to questions concerning governmental power. Points 71 through 87 present and refute the objections raised by the world. These are followed by point 88, which covers nearly two pages: "Since the [Church] Fathers at first also held that Christians may not go to war or serve as secular judges and that those in office were not regarded as Christians, let us look at some documents and testimonies that speak against their own practice."

Points 89 through 106 present further biblical evidence. In conclusion, the last point says significantly:

> The world has its laws; the Jews or the people of Moses had in their time their special system of laws over life and limb, far different from the world's system. Christians and their gospel also have their special system of laws and order given by Christ their King, not in accord with the Jewish law. For the kingdom of Christ is not physical but spiritual; it is a kingdom of peace and of the spiritual Melchizedek, where there is no strife nor lawsuit, nor use of the sword. Therefore the one must not be mixed with the other – the sword of the world put together with Moses and Christ, as the supposed Christians do. It is as harmonious as considering turnip greens and peas to be one and the same thing. O blindness and confusion!

Three years after Eberhard Arnold received this codex, he and the Rhön Bruderhof found themselves under a government that proved unequivocally the antithesis between the kingdom of Christ and the kingdom of the world. Arnold would use the Anabaptist interpretation given in "The Christian and the Sword" to develop his response to Adolf Hitler's rule of Germany.

Art Wiser, 2011

INTRODUCTION

BACKGROUND

"THE CHRISTIAN AND THE SWORD" is the fourth article of what is known as *The Great Article Book.*[1] It was written in the 1570s, at a time when a proliferating number of confessions of faith were at hand, and available for a new synthesis of where the Hutterites stood, on the basis of biblical theology. Five select points were decided upon, which together expressed elements within their faith that were deemed central and essential for an understanding of an Anabaptist faith from the Hutterian perspective. What eventuated served well both for instruction within: for internal use; and without: as a witness to interested individuals and individuals outside the Hutterian community. Four of these themes were basic to the preservation of the movement: believer's baptism, the Lord's Supper, community of goods, and the relationship of church and state. A fifth theme arose out of the mission program: the question of existing marriages between Hutterite converts and their non-Hutterite spouses.

The Great Article Book became the synthesizer and simplifier, in a format which all members could understand – five articles, around which the fundamental

Hutterian truths were built. This work reflects a new level within Hutterian history, which also parallels general European history of the 1570s and 80s: the age of confessionalism, and of a beginning orthodoxy.[2]

A typical Hutterian pattern of exegesis is developed within each of the five articles: a protracted analysis of Old and New Testament scriptures, including the apocryphal books, continuing with a series of polemical rejoinders, followed up with documentation from church history.

Since the work appeared anonymously, there has been some question among scholars as to its author. Peter Walpot, *Vorsteher* (head elder of the entire group), is probably the compiler, finalizing the task in 1577 of editing this collective work – which includes snippets from various earlier epistles and writings (verbatim from Leonhard Dax, but also from others). The earliest extant copy may well include, toward the end of each of the five articles, some addenda, added possibly by Hans Kräl, or even by the scribe, Hans Zuckenhammer, who inscribed on the title page: "Geschrieben von [in this case, 'copied by'] Hans Zuckenhammer, 1583."

The Great Article Book, although not published until 1967, was copied many times and served the community in many forms, consequently meriting a place alongside the printed Riedemann *Rechenschaft (Confession of Faith)* of the 1540s.

THE FOURTH ARTICLE: "CONCERNING THE SWORD"

THE FOURTH ARTICLE on the sword begins with Genesis and then wends its way through the biblical books until it reaches Revelation (points 66–69), at which juncture the high point of the article is reached, in a passage (point 70) collocating two realities which for the Hutterites defy correlation – two kingdoms, which differ as much as day and night. The point begins:

> Christians and the world are as different as heaven and earth. The world is world and remains world and acts like the world, and all the world is one world. The Christian, however, is called out of the world and is required no longer to conform to the world (John 15:19; 2 Cor. 6:14–18; Rev. 18:4; Rom. 12:2), no longer to be its consort (Eph. 5:6–7), no longer to walk in its disorderly confusion (1 Pet. 4:1–6), no longer to pull its yoke (2 Cor. 6:14–18). . . .

A reading of the whole point suggests a rugged Christian dualism, posed in bold relief. Discipleship is made possible through the process of the new birth (John 3), which demands leaving the realm of general society and entering an utterly other kingdom, ruled by Christ's spirit, where peace reigns. The notion that such peace could be fulfilled at all within the realm of the world is absolutely rejected; it can only be fulfilled through life in the Spirit of Christ. This same view is also expressed in point 38:

> ... To bear the cross is to accept suffering and sorrow, and even persecution, with patience. The sword does not suffer anything, but terminates everything in its path. Christians are counted as sheep for the slaughter. The sword is what kills them.

The question of war taxes is eloquently spoken to in point 56, a subject that came up regularly among the Hutterites, who were strongly opposed to such payment:

> Even if I personally did not want to be an arsonist, yet paid someone else for that purpose; even if I – to be precise, myself – did not want to do something, yet paid someone else to do it, and then authorized that person to go; indeed, if I were an enemy of a magistrate or ruling lord, yet did not want to strangle him with my own hands, but instead equipped and sent someone else to carry out this deed; would I then not be punished as a murderer, as if I had carried out the deed myself? Indeed, most certainly I would, and with good reason! In this same manner, and even more so, God will bring punishment upon someone who personally does not shed blood, but allows others to fight in war in his or her stead, compensating and supporting them. These alternatives are one and the same, and before God merit the same reward.

The rejection of private property for the Christian is spoken to throughout Article Three, but also surfaces in Article Four (including points 36, 94 and 101).

The Golden Rule (Matt. 7:12) finds its place in point 93, but its converse (which may also be found in Jewish literature) appears as well: "What you do not want done to you, don't do to your neighbor."

Article Four also speaks to the question of defending one's neighbor during a personal attack (point 102):

> Out of Christ's love come forbearance and love, hence we are not to injure anyone out of love for another; otherwise we abandon love for our enemies and miss the way of Christ, and only an outward alliance of mutual help as practiced in the whole world would result: If you help me, I will help you. But wherever true Christians can come to the aid of others in distress, be they friend or foe, if it can be given without injury to anyone, there it will never cease or be lacking among believers and followers of Christ because true Christian love injures nobody, neither friend nor foe.

And finally, nine times throughout the article, the phrase "kingdom of Christ" is used, certainly a phrase consciously chosen to underscore that Christians are tied to the New Testament Christ and his kingdom, and not to those Old Testament elements concerning the kingdom of God that came to an end (see points 9, 14, 17, 46, 62, 86, 88, 99, and 107). In this regard, a keen discernment into the nature and historical development of Christianity is tucked away in point 99:

> . . . As soon as worldly power mixed itself into the kingdom of Christ, the eating of blood (Ps. 16:4) – that

is, shedding the blood of man – began among supposed Christians, which the Holy Spirit now correctly forbids us to do as the children of God, whereby we need to be vigilant. If we do so, we do what is right.

SIGNIFICANCE FOR TODAY

THE QUESTION of the relationship of church and state is as acute today as it was in the 16th century; and on its deepest level is also tied inseparably to the question of the relationship of the New Testament to the Old. The nature of the state has changed in some major respects over the centuries, with various levels having been added from time to time, making things less clear-cut and thus more difficult to find appropriate handles for. Yet other levels of government remain equally sharply defined today, much as they did in the 1570s when the long article, "The Christian and the Sword," found its definitive form. Whether magistrates can be Christian may seem to have more shades of gray today, with the element of the welfare state having been added to the magisterial mix; but the questions of capital punishment, going to war, and protecting society are as much in the picture today as they were five centuries ago.

With this in mind, elements of "The Christian and the Sword," on the basis of biblical theology, speak as powerfully now as they did then – crucial themes that continue to trouble humankind in the very depths of its soul.

TRANSLATION PROCESS

ELIZABETH BENDER provided the original first draft of this translation. Emmy Barth Maendel and other members of the Bruderhof provided a typescript of Bender's original handwritten draft, incorporating the extensive framework of biblical references into the text itself and suggesting improvements in text throughout. The next step in the process was to check everything against the printed text,[3] and against a transcription of the whole made by Leonard Gross in 1966. Out of all this emerged an English translation in which the attempt was made to keep the meaning, spirit, and cadence of the original, but at the same time, transform all this into standard English. Many longer sentences in the original were so translated, where dividing them seemed to violate the original meaning. Translation of biblical passages are sometimes taken directly from the German, at other times (where the meaning permitted) taken from a modern English translation (the New Revised Standard Version, the Revised Standard Version, and at times, the King James Version). In a few places, differences between Friedmann's published German text (which is based on a 1597 codex in Berlin) and codex EAH 227 (see preface) are indicated in the notes.

Leonard Gross

In his days may righteousness flourish and peace
abound, till the moon be no more!
Psalm 72:7

But I say to you, "Do not resist one who is evil."
Matthew 5:39

But Jesus called to his disciples and said to them, "You
know that worldly rulers lord it over the nations,
and their great men rule with force.
It shall not be so among you."
Matthew 20:25–26

The powerful are called gracious lords, but not so with
you: the greatest among you shall become the least.
Luke 22:25–26

NONVIOLENCE IN THE OLD TESTAMENT

1 EARLY ON, GOD SAID to Noah, "For your lifeblood I shall surely require a reckoning; of every beast I will require it and of man; of every man's brother I will require the life of man. Whoever sheds the blood of man, by man shall his blood be shed; for God made man in his own image" (Gen. 9:5–6; Matt. 26:52; Rev. 13:10). Therefore God did not want a blood sacrifice, to indicate that if the blood of unreasoning beasts is so precious, how much more is that of a man!

2 KING DAVID PLANNED to build a house in honor of the name of the Lord his God. But the word of the Lord came to him, saying, "You may not build a house for my name, for you are a warrior and have shed blood. Lo, the son who will be born to you will be a man of peace. I will give him peace from his enemies round about, for his name shall be Solomon; for I will give peace and rest to Israel throughout his lifetime. He shall build a house to my name" (1 Chron. 28:3, 23:24–32, 29:1–30). This foreshadows the house of Christ as a wholly peaceable people, unspotted by bloodshed.

3 AND WHEN SOLOMON BUILT the house – the temple (which was to be a symbol or figure of the church of Christ in the New Testament) – it was built with undressed stone from the quarry, so that neither hammer nor axe nor any tool of iron was heard while the temple was being built (1 Kings 6:7). This foreshadows that the church of Christ shall not be brought to faith or built with noise or with force, as the papists do, together with their stepbrothers, who have handed over the gift of faith to kings and princes, allowing them to rule over faith with the sword and ramming it into the people.[4]

4 THE PEOPLE SAID TO SAMUEL, "Appoint us a king to govern us, like other nations, to go before us in battle and conduct our wars." This displeased Samuel, and the Lord said, "They have not rejected you, but they have rejected me from being king over them. They are now doing to you what they have always done from the day I brought them out of Egypt, up to this day; they have forsaken me and served other gods" (1 Sam. 8:5–8). If God was thus displeased with his earthly people Israel, what will he not do to us, to whom he sent his dearly beloved Son from heaven, had him appear on the earth and crowned him as our king. What if we were to forsake him, refuse to have him rule over us (Luke 19:14), and choose a fleshly arm to rule in his church, or even want to be king ourselves such as other nations have (Ps. 52:1–9)! For Christ is the only king in his church, and the word of the Lord is the only judge and sword of Christians.

Whoever rejects this and wants to have it otherwise, rejects not Christ but the Father who sent him, just as it was not Samuel who was rejected, but God. Here is one greater than Samuel, the fathers, and the prophets.

5 IN THE BOOK OF JUDGES we have a parable or analogy of this with the house of Gideon, who said to Israel, "I will not rule over you, and my son will not rule over you;[5] the Lord will rule over you" (Judg. 8:23). But Abimelech, the son of his concubine, proceeded to make himself king. Then Jotham, Gideon's son, said, "Listen to me, you men of Shechem, and may God listen to you: Once upon a time the trees came to anoint a king, and they said to the olive tree: 'Be king over us.' But the olive tree answered: 'What, leave my rich oil by which God and men are honored, to come and hold sway over the trees?' So the trees said to the fig tree: 'Then will you come and be king over us?' But the fig tree answered: 'What, leave my good fruit and all its sweetness, to come and hold sway over the trees?' So the trees said to the vine: 'Then will you come and be king over us?' But the vine answered: 'What, leave my new wine which gladdens gods and men to hold sway over the trees?' Then all the trees said to the thornbush: 'Will you then be king over us?' And the thornbush said to the trees: 'If you really mean to anoint me as your king, then come under the protection of my shadow; if not, fire shall come out of the thornbush and burn up the cedars of Lebanon'" (Judg. 9:7–15).

From this we see and learn that a Christian, who throughout the Scriptures is likened to an olive tree, fig tree, a vine and other good trees, can today so much the less be a ruler. If he does become a lord and ruler he forsakes his Christian fruit-bearing and has to go out to hold sway over the trees. For being a spiritual and Christian person cannot be combined with being a worldly power. The son of the concubine (who has no part in the inheritance with the legitimate son) is the government (Gal. 4:30). That is why government is likened to a thornbush as having the same nature, for it shares its nature. It is appointed, like wild trees, to tear, scratch, and prick. It is on account of these thorns that a ruler with thorns and claws is appointed to hold sway over others. But we, dear brethren, ought not to be so, but as Isaiah prophesies: Instead of the thorn shall come up the cypress; instead of the briar shall come up the myrtle (Isa. 55:13).

6 JACOB THE PATRIARCH also prophesied the same outcome, saying, "The scepter shall not depart from Judah until the hero (Christ) comes" (Gen. 49:10). Because the rulership of the Jews (who were at that time God's people) comes to an end in Christ, ceases, and is taken from them, it is indeed clear that the Jewish rule shall not exist in Christ and that he alone will rule among Christians with his spiritual sword. The fact that the power of the temporal sword is to be taken from the Jews means that henceforth, God's people shall no longer wield the sword, use it, or govern with it. And the fact

that it has been turned over to the heathen indicates that those who do not submit to the Spirit of Christ, that is, all the heathen and unbelievers, shall be subject to the rule and penalty of the sword, as it is written: "God has appointed that all nations have a government, but he alone has become Lord over Israel" (Sir. 17:17).

7 ISRAEL – THE JEWS as a figurative people – wielded the sword against its enemies, evildoers and opponents, nevertheless they did not move into battle without the Lord's orders and command (Num. 21:32–35; 20:14–29), but asked his counsel through his prophets and servants and heeded his word as to whether they should go to battle. When they failed to do this, marching out of their own free will (as happens today), they did not succeed, but at times suffered great humiliation and loss. Therefore, because the people of the New Testament have no command from the Lord to wage war – on the contrary, are forbidden to do so – on no account are they to take such a liberty.

8 JOB, THE GOD-FEARING MAN, says: "Be afraid of the sword, for wrath brings the punishment of the sword, that you may know there is a judgment" (Job 19:29). Therefore the temporal sword has been assigned to those who do not fear God and his final Judgment, so that they must learn to fear the sword and learn thereby, that while men punish with the sword, all the more will God punish at his Judgment. That is why Paul says, "The power of the

sword is given to be feared, not by those who do good, but by those who do evil" (Rom. 13:3).

9 DAVID, THE ROYAL PROPHET, prophesying of the church of Christ and describing the kingdom of Christ, says: "Come and see the works of the Lord, who has wrought such desolation on earth. He has made wars to cease to the ends of the earth (namely, through the gospel, which the apostles carried to all parts of the world, doing away with war among all believers). He has broken bows, shattered spears, and burned the chariots with fire" (Ps. 46:8–9).

10 "HIS ABODE HAS BEEN established in Salem, his dwelling place in Zion. There he broke the flashing arrows, the shield, the sword, and the weapons of war" (Ps. 76:2–3). Now, if man makes and prepares what God destroys, he is acting in direct opposition to God.

11 ISAIAH AND MICAH, two prophets, prophesy thus about the house and church of Christ: "Then the law will go forth from Zion and the word of the Lord from Jerusalem. He shall administer justice among the nations and arbitrate among many peoples, so that they shall beat their swords into plowshares, and their spears into pruning hooks, sickles and saws; no more will a nation take up arms against another nation nor will they learn war any more" (Isa. 2:3–4; Mic. 4:2–3). See how clearly the people of Christ will be such a peaceable people!

12 "THEN THE WOLF shall live with the sheep, and the leopard lie down with the kid; the calf and the young lion shall grow up together, and a little child shall lead them; the cow and the bear shall be friends, and their young shall lie down together. The lion shall eat straw like cattle. No one will harm or destroy another in my entire holy mountain" (Isa. 11:6–9; 65:25). That is how it will be in Christ, the branch of the tree of Jesse. And so he is saying that even the wolves will become friendly animals like sheep.

13 "THESE ARE THE WORDS of the Lord God, the Holy One of Israel: 'Come back, keep peace, and you will be safe. But you would have none of it'; you said, 'No, we will take horse and flee; therefore you shall be put to flight: We will ride apace; therefore swift shall be the pace of your pursuers'" (Isa. 30:15–16). Likewise false Christians even today continue to disobey and say the same things. Therefore the same thing will happen to them.

14 "WHERE PREVIOUSLY dragons dwelt, reeds and rushes will grow. . . . No lion shall come there, no savage beast climb onto it, but one shall walk freely and safely" (Isa. 35:7,9). Dragons and beasts of prey that bare their teeth at one another and dare to eat another represent the poisonous, tyrannical people who use the sword and have swords for teeth (Prov. 30:14); they will no longer exist in the kingdom of Christ.

15 "ALL YOUR CHILDREN shall be taught by God, to whom I shall give abiding peace. In righteousness you shall be established, dwelling far away from violence" (Isa. 54:13–14).

16 "I WILL APPOINT PEACE as your overseer and Righteousness as your taskmaster. The sound of violence shall no more be heard in your land, nor devastation or destruction within your borders" (Isa. 60:17–18); for all your peoples will fear God.

17 "THE WOLF AND THE LAMB shall feed together, and the lion shall eat straw like cattle, but the food of the snake shall be dust. No one shall harm or kill another in my entire holy mountain, says the Lord" (Isa. 65:25). So where there is beating, lashing, stabbing, shooting, injuring one another, laying to ruin, quarreling, fighting, killing and shedding blood, that is the devil's ungodly and unclean mountain and Lucifer's place. For just as one recognizes the kingdom of Christ and his disciples by their love, peace, and unity, so also the devil's kingdom by the wrangling, quarreling, and warring of those who take after Cain.

18 JEREMIAH THE PROPHET SAYS: "Thus says the Lord: . . . Tell the king and the mighty: 'Give up your power and be like the common people, for your proud crowns will fall from your heads'" (Jer. 13:18). All the more must this take place today in Christendom if they want to repent and become Christians.

19 EZEKIEL PROPHESIED: "Behold, it comes; it shall be, says the Lord God, the day of which I have spoken. The dwellers in the cities of Israel shall come out and gather weapons to light their fires, buckler and shield, bow and arrows, throwing-stick and lance, and they shall kindle fires with them for seven years. They will not need to take wood from the field or cut down any in the forests. They will have enough weapons to light their fires" (Ezek. 39:8–10). How then can the people of Christ be rulers who use weapons of vengeance, when the people of Christ have rooted out and stopped using weapons of wrath and of vengeance, lifelong? (That is the meaning of the seven years). If weapons of bloodshed are to be rooted out and burned, what will become of those who cannot make enough of them?

20 DANIEL PROPHESIES concerning the end-time, the time of the Antichrist, that those who are willing to acknowledge his God will prevail and lead the way. And so the wise among God's people will give the church understanding and will have to struggle for a long time through fire, through prison, and through robbery (Dan. 11:32–33). Note here who the ruler will be; note also that the wise will fall victim to the sword and fire – not that they will kill anyone, or use the sword, or take vengeance.[6]

21 HOSEA WRITES that the Lord says: "I will have pity on the house of Judah, and I will deliver them by the Lord their God; I will not deliver them by bow, nor by sword, nor by war, nor by horses, nor by horsemen" (Hosea 1:7). "I will abolish the bow, the sword, and war from the land; and I will make them dwell in safety" (Hosea 2:18).

22 "O ISRAEL, you have destroyed yourself; but in me is your help. Where are your kings who were to help you in all your cities? Where are your rulers and protectors who were to save you? For you said, 'Give us a king and prince.' In my anger I gave you a king, and in my fury I took him away" (Hosea 13:9–11). Thus God gave men rulers simply out of anger as is seen here in Israel's case. "For the Lord said: 'It is I whom they have rejected, I whom they will not accept as their king'" (1 Sam. 8:7). Because they then forsook God and wanted to have a king like all the nations, he gave them one and fulfilled their desire, to their own harm, so that his Spirit would not always have to contend with men, for they were flesh (Gen. 6:3). What God ordered and gave in wrath is neither fitting nor appropriate in Christ, in whom there is blessing and mercy, and the child of blessing cannot be the servant of wrath and revenge. For God's intention for us was not to inherit wrath, but to inherit blessedness through Jesus Christ (1 Thess. 5:9).

23 JONAH THE PROPHET began by going a day's journey into the city of Nineveh, proclaiming to the Ninevites: "'In forty days Nineveh shall be overthrown!' And the people of Nineveh believed God's word. They proclaimed a public fast and put on sackcloth from the greatest to the least of them. When the news reached the king of Nineveh he rose from his throne, stripped off his robes of state, put on sackcloth and sat in ashes. Then he issued a proclamation to all of Nineveh: 'By the decree of the king and his nobles, let neither man nor beast, herd nor flock, taste anything; let them not taste food, or graze, or drink water, but let man and beast be covered with sackcloth and call on God without ceasing. Let everyone turn from his evil ways and his habitual acts of arrogance and violence. It may be that God will again be gracious, and turn away from his fierce anger, that we not perish'" (John 3:4–9). And that is what happened. The only sign that will be given this wicked and adulterous generation, said Christ, is the sign of Jonah (Matt. 12:39); if they want to repent they must descend from their thrones and forsake worldly pomp and splendor. How, then, is a Christian to ascend the throne in the first place?

24 ZECHARIAH SAYS: "REJOICE GREATLY, O daughter of Zion, be glad, daughter of Jerusalem; for see, your king, the Just One, the Savior, is coming to you. He is humble and lowly, riding on an ass, on a foal, the young of a she-ass. He shall banish chariots of war from Ephraim and war horses from Jerusalem; the warrior's bow shall be banished. He shall proclaim laws of peace to the nations and his rule shall extend from sea to sea, from the River to the ends of the earth" (Zech. 9:9–10).

25 EZRA THE PROPHET, upon receiving from God the secret knowledge of the end-time (how it will be with Christ and his followers), says: "I saw a man who waxed strong with the clouds of heaven; wherever he turned his eyes, all things they fell upon trembled. And whenever a voice proceeded from his mouth, all that heard him were burned up like dry kindling that is ignited. Then I saw that many people assembled, so many that no one could count them. They came from the four winds of heaven to make war on the man who arose out of the sea. Then he hewed out a high mountain and flew on to it. Then I saw that all who had assembled to make war on him were terrified, and yet they dared to fight. But when he saw the attack and the violence of the crowd, however, he raised neither hand nor blade (note, neither hand nor blade) indeed, no weapon at all; but he blew a blast like fire from his mouth, and from his lips a flame, and from his tongue a storm of sparks. All these things combined, and fell with fury upon the people that had armed themselves to attack him, and consumed them with fire, so that nothing was to be seen but dust and ashes and smoke. Then I saw the same man descend from the mountain and call unto himself another, peaceable people" (note, Christ will call and prepare a peaceable people for himself – not like the first Israelites, but one that like him, raises neither hand, sword, nor any other weapon), "and many nations came to him; some were joyful, some fearful, some enslaved, and they were brought before him" (2 Esd. 13:3–12).

This was interpreted to Ezra thus: "The man whom you saw is the one whom God Most High has kept for a long time; he will himself set his creation free";[7] truly the Son of God will be revealed and will punish the nations that have assembled for their wickedness. He will, without exertion, simply destroy them through the word that is likened unto the fire (Heb. 4:12) which Paul calls the sword of the Spirit (Eph. 6:17), and John in Revelation calls the sword of his mouth (Rev. 1:16; 19:15). The peaceable nation, however, is the ten tribes that Salmanasser, the King of Assyria, led away captive from their homeland. Hereby, by way of hidden allegory, he indicates the people of Christ in the end time, who have been ensnared into Babylonian and Assyrian captivity and released by Christ, and will henceforth be peacemakers and a peaceable people who will never engage in warfare, the shedding of blood, secular courts, or the use of the sword or violence.

NONVIOLENCE IN THE GOSPELS

26 CHRIST, THE PRINCE OF PEACE (Isa. 9:6), teaches us this gospel, saying: Blessed are the meek, blessed are the merciful, blessed are the peacemakers, blessed are those who are persecuted for righteousness' sake (Matt. 5:5, 7, 9, 10). From this it follows that the arrogant and surly are unchristian and unblessed, the unmerciful are unblessed, the war makers and those who quarrel are unblessed, those who cause persecution are unblessed. For that reason, whoever exercises the office of the sword cannot be in Christ. Whoever carries the sword at his side is not a peacemaker but a combat maker.

27 CHRIST SAYS: "You have heard that it was said to the men of old, 'You shall not kill,'" (now this command includes assaulting, for assaulting is killing at heart), "and 'whoever kills shall be liable to judgment.' But I say to you that every one who is angry with his brother shall be liable to judgment; whoever insults his brother shall be liable to the council, and whoever says 'you fool!' shall be liable to the hell of fire" (Matt. 5:21–22). Now, if a Christian is not to be angry with his brother nor call him a fool without deserving eternal fire, how would it be possible for him to wield the sword, even to kill him, or attack anyone in body or soul or help another to do so? No Christian may do this.

But if you say, then nobody could be safe from robbers and enemies: Answer: What do you and I have to do with the world (1 Cor. 5:12), since we want to be Christians? We are now speaking of true Christians, not of the heathen and Jews. It does not befit a Christian to condemn to death. These verses do not apply to worldly authorities nor the heathen nor to the Jews, but only to true Christians. For the judgment that Christ has given and commanded us is not applicable to outsiders who are not members of the church (*gmain*). Whoever wants to be a secular ruler, let him be one, and whoever wants to be a Christian, let the person be a Christian.

28 FURTHER SAYS CHRIST: "You have heard that it was said 'An eye for an eye and a tooth for a tooth.' But I say to you" (the Christians), "Do not resist one who is evil. But if anyone strikes you on the right cheek, turn to him the other also" (that is, rather than avenge yourself and return blow for blow, you should suffer still more); "and if anyone would sue you and take your coat, let him have your cloak as well" (Matt. 5:38–40). Now, if Christians did not sue at law, so also has conducting court trials, or being a judge, fallen away of itself and been discontinued in Christendom. All this clearly shows, since he has taken away occasion and cause for a secular court, that he has forbidden and done away with such things among all of his own. He will not have his people of the New Testament resist evil with revenge, sword, and bloodshed. Nor will he have them make a legal demand for corporal punishment – this is expressly forbidden them, for there is to be no eye for an eye or hand for a hand in his church. On the contrary, one must consider whether God's law has been broken and treat a transgressor in accord with what he deserves, that is, in accord with the gospel, which has the ban only and no sword, the force of the keys and not the force of the executioner like the world.

But someone may say, If all of us put away our swords and did what you do and say, who would resist the Turks and enemies? Answer: If everyone were Christian, it would be God who would resist the enemy. For he alone is the protection of his little church; otherwise they would be devoured by enemies like bread.

29 FURTHER SAYS CHRIST: "You have heard that it was said, 'You shall love your neighbor and hate your enemy.' But I say to you, love your enemies and speak kindly to those who persecute you; do good to those who hate you" (Matt. 5:43–44). Thus the office of government and the power of the sword is in itself in all matters the contrary and opposite of the words and statements of Christ. Consequently, there can be no Christian government nor can a Christian hold such an office. For it is impossible for two mutually contradictory things to be reconciled. But in the world, which does not live according to God's will, government is as necessary as daily bread. So we should hold it in honor, and be subject to it in all that is good.

30 CHRIST TEACHES his followers to pray to God: "Forgive us our debts as we forgive our debtors" (Matt. 6:12; Luke 11:4). The apostle teaches: "Forgive one another. As Christ has forgiven you, so you also must forgive" (Col. 3:13). But if we requite evil and injury with the sword, with killing, with imprisonment and similar revenge, and pray God to forgive us as we forgive these actions, we will be praying for death, for the sword and prison, and revenge upon ourselves. That is why Christ says: All who take the sword will perish by the sword, and he who imprisons will be put in prison. That is what such people are asking for and praying for daily, in the Lord's Prayer. Therefore, he who does not forgive his brother draws the sword upon himself like a senseless madman. He is prescribing his own punishment and passing sentence upon himself. It does not fit together and is like black and white.

31 "JUDGE NOT," SAYS CHRIST to his followers, "that you be not judged. For with the judgment you pronounce, you will be judged, and the measure you give will be the measure you get" (Matt. 7:1–2). Therefore, the sword, judgment, and vengeance can never be mixed into the church, nor can any Christian wield and administer them.

32 CHRIST SAYS, "Go and learn what this means, 'I desire mercy, and not sacrifice.' I have come to call sinners to repentance" (Matt. 9:13). Therefore Christ wants mercy and grace on earth among his people, and not wrath and the sword. For Christians are not to nurse anger or hatred toward anyone on earth, not to mention protecting oneself with the sword. For in heaven there is neither envy nor hatred. For if there were envy and hatred in heaven, the earth would long since have perished, the sea long since drained away, and there would not be a drop of blood left on earth. But because it is the nature of heaven to do good to those who injure them, so Christ wants his people to take on that kind of manner and nature. Therefore he has taught us to pray: "Thy will be done on earth as it is in heaven" (Matt. 6:10).

33 CHRIST IS THE LAMB OF GOD (John 1:29) and was led like a lamb to the slaughter (Isa. 53:7). A lamb never tears a wolf to pieces. Therefore he says to his people, "Behold, I send you out as sheep in the midst of savage wolves; so be wise as the serpent" (Matt. 10:16), which offers itself up and heeds little how its body is cut up as long as its head remains whole. We likewise are to care little about the loss of other things, even our bodies, if only we keep our faith, which is the head and the root. We should therefore be like amiable, nonresistant, and long-suffering lambs, and for that reason we are called sheep (John 10). But those who are armed with horns and have the characteristics of goats are called goats

(Matt. 25), and are the ungodly who are equipped for butting back.

34 "DO NOT FEAR THOSE who kill the body, but who cannot kill the soul" (Matt. 10:28). If there were supposed to be a government wielding the sword in the Christian church of God as there is today in the false Christendom of the world, Christ would hardly have needed to speak those words. For Christians could then have fled behind the sword and fight back and strike the enemy's throat as quickly as the enemy could strike theirs. But the words actually declare that Christians (true Christians I mean) are killed, tortured, imprisoned, and persecuted in the world. But they absolutely never kill, or imprison, or persecute anyone. How then could they be secular rulers?

35 ALL THE EVANGELISTS TESTIFY that Christ prophesied of the Christians: "They will deliver you up to the councils, and flog you in their synagogues, and they will drag you before governors and kings for my sake" (Matt. 10:17–18; Matt. 24:9; Luke 21:12). "They will put you out of the synagogues; indeed, the hour is coming when whoever kills you will think he is doing service to God" (John 16:2). Note again whether rulers can be Christians. For this is happening today just as in earlier times.

36 CHRIST GIVES THE APOSTLES in his church the power of the keys, as he says to Peter: "I will give you the keys of the kingdom of heaven" (Matt. 16:19). Likewise he says to all of them: "Receive the Holy Spirit. If you forgive the sins of any, they are forgiven; if you retain the sins of any, they are retained" (Matt. 18:15–18; John 20:22–23). This power Christ gave his apostles and his church. But the power of the sword he did not give to any apostle or disciple, nor to anyone in his church. You would have to search until you died to find it in the New Testament. The ban, ordained for the church of Christ, and the sword, ordained for the world, are as different as night and day, they are as incomprehensibly different as life and death. Hence they cannot be combined.

The power of the keys, the Christian ban, removes from the church what is evil (1 Cor. 5:5). The worldly sword removes completely from the earth. The Christian punishment is love, indeed, a brotherly reproof; the punishment of the sword is wrath and ruthlessness. After the ban of Christians one can repent; but after the sword or worldly justice, penitence and reform are forever cut off. The ministers of the keys are the vessels of mercy, the ministers of the worldly sword are the vessels of wrath (Rom. 9:16–18; Hos. 13:11). He who applies and holds the power of the keys over the Christian brotherhood banishes greed and private ownership. He who holds the power of the sword over greed and property (Acts 5:1; 1 Cor. 5:1–13) has his own land and people; hence from time immemorial the power of the sword has been identified by the name, "the worldly government." That is why its office cannot be fitted into the unadulterated Christian church. For each walks its own way; the paths go in opposite directions and never meet.

37 IN THE PARABLE of the tares, when the servants said: "Do you want us to go and pull them out?", the Lord answered: "No, lest in gathering the tares you root up the wheat along with them. Let both grow together until the harvest" (Matt. 13:28–29). Christ said this because he wanted to prevent wars and bloodshed among his people, as almost the entire fifth chapter of Matthew shows. He does not forbid removing the evildoers and tares from his church by the power of the keys, but removing them with the sword. Killing and executing them is what he forbids, lest the tares that might still be transformed into good grain be thereby cut off.

38 CHRIST SAYS to his disciples: "If any man would come after me, let him deny himself and take up his cross and follow me" (Matt. 16:24). He does not say "take up the sword," "for the sword has absolutely no place next to the cross, and Christ cannot agree with Belial. Hence the worldly sword and the cross of Christ are as alike as Christ and Pilate. They get along together like wolves and sheep in one stall. The friends of the sword cannot be anything but enemies of Christ's cross. And the teaching of the sword is contrary to the teaching of the cross, which must be witnessed to by bearing the cross and not with fighting back. To bear the cross is to accept suffering and sorrow, and even persecution, with patience. The sword does not suffer anything, but terminates everything in its path. Christians are counted as sheep for the slaughter (Ps. 44:23; Rom. 8:36; 2 Cor. 4:11). The sword is what kills them.

39 WHEN THE DISCIPLES CAME to Jesus and said, "Who is the greatest in the kingdom of heaven?", Jesus called a child and put him in the midst of them: "Truly I say to you, unless you turn and become like children, you will never enter the kingdom of heaven" (Matt. 18:1–3). With this he wants to forbid, and remove from among his disciples, all rulership, domination, violence, sword and wrongdoing. For the souls of small children are pure of all temptations; they desire no revenge upon those who have injured them but, as if nothing had happened, they turn back to the people as to their friends. Yes, what child is greater than another? If a thousand were together, not one of them would know of a lord, a master, or a mayor; they are all on the same level and none is special as long as they are children.

Therefore, we as God's children need to be and become like innocent children, without domination, without vengeance, without pride, not domineering, not vengeful, not pompous – all these things stand in the way of our salvation. Take note, secular authorities! If you ask whether you can be Christians, the answer is given by the Son of God himself: "Unless you turn and become like children, you will never enter the kingdom of heaven."

That has to take place; you must demonstrate a turning if you want to be Christians.

40 THE LORD BECAME very angry at the man who seized his fellow man by the throat and threw him into prison for the debt that he owed. The Lord called him a wicked servant and delivered him to the torturers (Matt. 18:23–34). With this parable he declares that he does not want such a thing among his people in Christendom.

41 WHEN THE TWO SONS of Zebedee appealed to Christ and asked to be seated in his kingdom, the one to his right and the other to his left (Matt. 20:20–21), thus wanting the upper and most honorable seats (since they understood it to be a worldly and temporal kingdom because they were still immature), Christ deflected them away from that desire and warned them of the sweat, struggle, and suffering to come, that they would have to drink his cup and be baptized with his baptism. Hence Christians cannot occupy governmental positions, but must drink the cup of suffering on earth (Matt. 26:39) and be baptized with the baptism of anxiety (Luke 12:50).

42 JESUS CALLED HIS DISCIPLES and said to them: "You know that secular rulers lord it over the nations and their great men coerce them, but it shall not be so among you" (Matt. 20:25–26; Luke 22:25–26). You see, he thereby ties a firm knot that cannot be untied or undone. For he mentions the government and the lords of the world and says expressly, "It shall not be so among you, my people. The overlords proceed with coercion; it shall not be so among you; whoever will be great among you must be your servant; whoever will be the most prestigious among you must be your slave, even as the Son of Man came not to be served but to serve" (Mark 10:42–43). There will always be a flawed, earthly splendor, and it would be not at all fitting, when Christ lived as a poor slave, for us disciples to desire to be "gracious lords."

Therefore, in Christendom it shall not be like the rulers of this world who have authority on earth, each one above the other. One is the chief marshal, another the deputy marshal, another the mayor, another the chancellor, another this, another that. "It shall not be so among you," says Christ. With this statement Christ does not abolish temporal government, but leaves it in the world. He abolishes it from among his disciples and Christians; they shall not use force nor have jurisdiction over life and death. There shall therefore be as little worldly lordship among them as there is in heaven – that is to say, there is to be none at all among Christians on the earth. For if Lucifer had to be cast out because he wanted to be above others in heaven, how much more will those be cast out on earth who are guilty of such heathen deeds, which means they cannot be Christians.

Luke says that those in authority over them are called "gracious lords, but it must not be so among you" (Luke 22:25–26). For nothing leads to pride like the desire to rule and be the chief; great abominations have sprung from this, for human honors and prestige lead to much more that is shameful. Wanton honor makes men puffed up, irresponsible blasphemers and hypocrites. Splendor removes the bridle from their eyes and opens to them the door to hell, as if in a violent storm their spirit were turned around, overturning their boat into the depths of the water.

But it is not our will or intention to abolish temporal government or to be disobedient in all good and proper things. For there shall and must be government on earth among men, just as a school teacher must have a rod for disobedient children. For since the world and heathen nations do not fear God, nor allow themselves to be ruled by his Spirit and are thus without God's order, government with the sword is prescribed among them to be feared, as children fear the teacher's rod, to prevent complete chaos, and the earth from becoming completely stained with blood. The world still needs to preserve a worldly piety, like a horse in an emergency stall, a wolf in a pit, or a lion and bear on a chain.

43 CHRIST CALLS worldly government and force the gates of hell (Matt. 16:18). For just as Christ is the door and gate to God's kingdom (John 10:7, 9), they are called the gates of hell. As one can see, if the king, prince or authority is papist, then his subjects must also be papist; if he becomes Lutheran, they must also become Lutheran; if he is Zwinglian, they must also be Zwinglian; and what the government believes, its land and people must also believe. They enforce this with the sword, the hangman, fire and water, tower and dungeon, and so it happens that one believes in order to please another and goes with the crowd; everyone believes whatever his lord wishes. According to how the wind blows for the ruler, that is the direction the world takes, entering through such gates of hell with an ungodly, wicked life. That is why Christ also calls it the power of darkness (Luke 22:53); Paul calls it the dominion of darkness, and the rulers of this present darkness in this world against whom the God-fearing must contend (Col. 1:13; Eph. 6:12).[8]

44 "IF ANYONE WILL NOT RECEIVE you, leave the place" says Christ, "and shake the dust from your feet" in response (Matt. 10:14). See, Christians have this command. It does not say, proceed against them with the sword (like the greedy false prophets, teachers of war, and doctors of hangmen, that is, learned judges and priests of this world are wont to do); for nowhere is there a word about the apostles or Christ laying violent hands on anyone, but violent hands are laid on them. No one should dare to fight with the sword for the sake of his faith or God's justice, for if God wanted that, and rods and violence had to be used, he would no doubt send down from heaven his legion of angels (Matt. 26:53). Therefore, those who falsely attempt to spread the kingdom of God on earth by force are acting contrary to God's command and example. For it is not given to all (2 Thess. 3:2), but only to the chosen; we do not call compelled people believers. When John the Baptist came (John 3:23), he did not strike at the people with a sword but said, "Bear fruits that befit repentance" (Matt. 3:8 and elsewhere).

45 WHEN THE PHARISEES tempted him and showed him the tax coin, the Lord said, "Render to Caesar the things that are Caesar's and to God the things that are God's" (Matt. 22:21). Therefore it is Christ's will that his people, in subjection to worldly authority, give and offer its dues – what belongs to it – for the sake of its office and God's order. We may give it its due, and what belongs to God we are to give to God. But if men tamper with God's word and glory, acting contrary to it, we must faithfully keep that for God. For governments are lords only over what is physical, not over word and Spirit. That is why Paul also says, "Give all men their dues, taxes to whom taxes are due, revenue to whom revenue is due, respect to whom respect is due, honor to whom honor is due" (Rom. 13:7). But if you hear that you should give the emperor the things that are the emperor's, you should know without a doubt that the things are to be understood as only those that do not sully the faith, and that do not injure piety and religion or the conscience. For whatever is detrimental to faith and virtue is tribute paid not to the emperor but to the devil. For slaying and killing is the nature and work of the devil; he was a murderer from the beginning (John 8:44) and instigates wars in the world. A Christian cannot assist in this, for we have the reputation that we are called Christians. And since we bear the name of Christ, we are to do absolutely nothing that is contrary to a Christian life.

46 "WHEN HIS DISCIPLES entered a village in Samaria to spend the night at an inn, and the people refused to admit them, his disciples James and John said, 'Lord, do you want us to bid fire come down from heaven and consume them, as Elijah did?' Then Jesus turned and rebuked them and said, 'Do you not know what manner of spirit you are of? For the Son of Man came not to destroy men's lives but to save them'" (Luke 9:54–55; 2 Kings 1:10). Hence, his followers cannot destroy anyone. Not many words are needed; it is obvious that revenge has no place in the kingdom of Christ and that a Christian can neither engage in warfare and revenge nor contribute to such activities. How then can he hold a government office? Whoever does so has forsaken and denied Christ and Christ's way.

It does no good to say, David was a king and many pious men have exercised the power of the sword and gone to war. When the disciples cited Elijah as an example, Christ rebuked them, refusing to allow it, and said: "Do you not know what manner of spirit you are of?" Therefore you cannot say: He who had the Spirit of God has also the Spirit of Christ. For here Christ admonishes the disciples to distinguish between his Spirit and that of Elijah or of the people of the Old Testament, between the spirit of Christians and that of the world (Ps. 51:12). Therefore Paul says, "We have received not the spirit of the world, but the Spirit which is from God" (1 Cor. 2:12). Christ says that the world cannot receive the Spirit of truth, because it neither sees nor knows him. "But you," he says, "know him, for he dwells with you and will be in you" (John 14:17).

Herein can one recognize the Spirit of God: the fruit of the Spirit (says Paul) is love, joy, peace, patience, kindness, goodness, faithfulness, gentleness, self-control (Gal. 5:22–23). The fruit of the spirit of the world is hatred, disunity, enmity, strife, envy, wrath, fighting, quarreling, divisions, murder, drunkenness, gluttony, and the like. The Holy Spirit loathes and flees from hypocrites who merely pretend to be disciplined and wise (Wisd. of Sol. 1:5). Where evil takes the upper hand, the Spirit departs and refuses to constantly bicker with them. But the spirit of the world loathes those who withdraw from evil and hates those who no longer go along with its unruly crowd (Gen. 6:3).

The spirit of Christians is a steadfastly gentle and quiet spirit (1 Pet. 3:4); the spirit of the world is a fickle, rough spirit of gambling and poltergeists, yes, a vengeful spirit. But the Lord is not there, he is neither with it nor in it; as the Lord showed the prophet Elijah an indication of this difference when he bade him go to the mountaintop. Then the Lord passed by, and "a great and strong wind rent the mountain and broke in pieces the rocks before the Lord, but the Lord was not in the wind; and after the wind came an earthquake, but the Lord was not in the earthquake; and after the earthquake came a fire, but the Lord was not in the fire; and after the fire there came a still small voice" – and there was the Lord (1 Kings 19:11–12).

Christians have a new heart and a new spirit which God gives and implants in their innermost being (Ps. 68; Ezek. 11:19; 36:26). And all drink of one Spirit (1 Cor. 12:13). But old wine skins that cannot hold the new wine (Matt. 9:17 and elsewhere) and do not have Christ's Spirit are not his (Rom. 8:9). Therefore we have to distinguish and note whose spirit we are children of (Luke 9:55): not of the world, or of the spirit of evil, who is now at work in the children of unbelief, among whom we all once lived according to the will of the flesh and of reason (Eph. 2:3), but of Christ's Spirit, yea, the Spirit of the New Testament that practices no vengeance or destruction of human souls, but always seeks their salvation and preservation.

47 WHEN ONE OF THE MULTITUDE said to Jesus, "Master, bid my brother divide the inheritance with me," Jesus said to him, "Man, who has made me a judge or divider over you?" (Luke 12:13–14). It was as though he meant to say, "In what way does your quarreling over temporal things concern me? I did not come and was not sent to judge such matters." For whoever seeks earthly things does not seek what is in Christ, and therefore cannot get a ruling from him. Likewise no pupil or disciple of his who wants to be Christian can hold a judicial office or be a judge over temporal things. But he who

dares to do this does not have the mind of Christ but the mind of the world. The apostle, however, says, "We have the mind of Christ" (1 Cor. 2:16).

48 WHEN JESUS PERCEIVED that the people were about to come and take him by force to make him king, he escaped and fled (John 6:15). He did this in part as a precedent and example for us. For he who has chosen all the simple things (1 Cor. 1:27–28) – mother, home, fatherland, food, clothing – yes, also calls the simple and lowly of the world (for what is exalted among men is an abomination to God (Luke 16:15) also desires that we follow in his footsteps. For, as the apostle says, those whom he called he has predestined to be conformed to the image of his son (Rom. 8:29). Whoever acts otherwise reviles the footsteps of Christ (Ps. 89:51). From this it is clear that a person who wants to be a worldly ruler does not have the Spirit of Christ. If he does not have the Spirit of Christ he is by no means a Christian; if he had the Spirit, he would leave the office, since no Christian can be a worldly ruler. But if you want to be a king, I will show you a realm – govern yourself, keep yourself under good control, and you will be a true king. For he who can govern and conquer himself is the greatest and most powerful of kings.

49 CHRIST REFUSED to condemn to death or pass judgment on the woman caught in adultery (John 8:11) although the law upholds such judgment.

Neither can a Christian do so with God's approval even though the office of the ruler demands it. For "just as the Father sent me into the world," says Christ, "so send I you" (John 17:18; 20:21). If Christ was not sent into the world to reign as a worldly king, prince or lord, or an authority using force, sword and splendor, much less are we. For he says "the servant shall not be greater than his lord, nor the messenger than he who sent him" (John 13:16); it is enough if he is like his master.

50 THE GOVERNMENT is an outward servant of law, of vengeance. "The servant does not continue in the house forever," says Christ (John 8:35), and cannot participate in the joy and inheritance of his master, and be saved unless he become one of the children. "Cast out this slave woman with her son," says the Scripture, "for the son of this slave woman shall not be heir with my son Isaac" (Gen. 21:10, 12; Gal. 4:30). Hence they cannot boast of anything more than citizenship on earth. With the rich man they are receiving good things here, and have their portion and their reward in this life (Luke 16:25), and cannot look forward to the hope of heaven unless they turn away from the slavery of the law and become children of light and the gospel, yes, from the worldly to the Christian. For two heavens they will not be able to have.

51 "MY KINGDOM is not of this world," said Christ to Pilate, "otherwise my servants would stand and fight and contend for me" (John 18:36). Thus, our King, Jesus Christ, is a spiritual king and has a spiritual realm. Therefore his sword must not be physical but spiritual. A spiritual kingdom cannot employ a physical sword. For worldly rulers wield a physical sword, since their realm is also physical. Therefore all who would defend themselves with force and the sword are certainly not of the realm of Christ. For his servants do not position themselves thus, as he himself says here. And because his reign is not of this world, but the government is worldly, the two can neither merge nor be alike. And those who quarrel, battle and fight for the kingdom of this world indicate clearly that they are not Christians, for the kingdom of this world is the devil's realm; he is a prince of this world, as Christ says (John 12:31).

52 WHEN THEY LED JESUS to the brow of the hill, and intended to throw him down headlong, he passed through the midst of them and went away (Luke 4:29–30). It does not say he attacked them, even though he often had many people with him, five thousand and seven thousand; he could even have annihilated them with a word and dry them up like the fig tree. But he offered no resistance. Paul also tells how he had suffered much at the hands of those who refused to believe him, namely, five times he received lashes, and was beaten with rods and stoned. It does not say that he defended himself even once, or that the churches, some of which were large, arose and defended or protected themselves with the sword. Oh no! If the apostles had precipitated an uproar and violently struck out at Christ's enemies with the sword and conquered Jerusalem, compelling everybody to accept their faith, what would that have been but damnation to their souls. It is therefore a devilish defense and unchristian.

53 THE HOLY SPIRIT CAME in the form of a dove (Matt. 3:16 and elsewhere), sent upon the believers (Acts 2:4) not in the form of a griffon or other beast of prey. A dove (which has no gall or bitterness) does not fall upon a falcon or hawk or eagle, nor does it attack any other bird. The dove is among birds what the sheep is among animals, which has no wish to injure any animal, but is attacked by them – persecuted, attacked and killed by eagles, hawks, ravens and additional birds of the falcon family and other hostile birds.

THE APOSTLES ON NONVIOLENCE

54 THE APOSTLE PAUL WRITES that we should not be conformed to this world, but be transformed by the renewal of our mind (Rom. 12:2). Now the most common characteristic of the world is to bear and use swords and other weapons of death, which no member of Christ should do. But government must be conformed to this world if it wants to govern, and it does whatever is the practice in this world and leads the course of the world. Therefore it has the status of temporal power. It is of the world, yes, the summit of worldly power, of which it is the chief expression. To this, Christians should not be conformed, as Paul says. Therefore a Christian cannot be a worldly ruler.

55 "REPAY NO MAN EVIL FOR EVIL," says Paul (Rom. 12:17). But it is the office of government to repay evil for evil (Rom. 13:4). "Do not be haughty but be humble" (Rom. 12:16). But the government is very haughty and must be in a lofty position because it is the government of the world. That is another reason why no Christian can rule. If possible, so far as it depends on you, live peaceably with all men (Rom. 12:18). Beloved, avenge not yourselves, but leave it to the wrath of God, for it is written, "Vengeance is mine, I will repay, says the Lord" (Deut. 32:35).

But worldly authority must avenge itself if it wants to be the government of the world. That is never the duty of the Christian. On the contrary, as Paul says further (Rom. 12:20): "If your enemy is hungry, feed him; if he is thirsty, give him drink" (Rom. 12:20). Thus God permits the Christian no sword or vengeance. For if servants quarrel among themselves and do not respect their masters but make bold to avenge themselves even after their masters have pled with them, their masters not only refuse to accept them but become angry and rebuke them as disgraceful and dishonorable rogues and tell them what they ought to have known.

Thus, if your servant undertakes to avenge himself, you, his master, will be harsh with him. So much the more God, who admonishes us, will say that we should give all that over to him. For what could be more unreasonable than that we, if we demand such modesty of our servants, refuse to render it to our Lord God? Therefore, if someone has grieved you, you are not to try to grieve him in return, or you will be like him and gain nothing.

No one can overcome one evil with another; on the contrary, evil is overcome by good (Rom. 12:21). For it is not suffering insult that is an evil, but offering insult, or the inability to endure it. Therefore David says: "The helpless commit themselves to you; you have been the helper of the orphan" (Ps. 10:14). Thus, the ungodly man has his judge without you, and you, man of God, shall not want to wantonly ascribe to yourself the honor of the only-begotten son (1 Thess. 4).

Vengeance and judgment are reserved for this Judge alone. But if you, out of ambition to judge, should want to be a judge, I will show you a judge's seat. On it is seated your spirit and mind, a judge over your soul and conscience: why did you dare to do this and that, and why did you neglect this and that? Then punish yourself, and you will have enough of the office of judgment.

56 "LET EVERY MAN," says Paul (and he does not exclude the believers to whom he is writing) "be subject to the authorities" (Rom. 13:1). He does not say that they should or could be authorities of power but says to be subject. "For there is no government except from God. But the authority that exists everywhere" (note, everywhere – thus he refers not only to the Roman and supposedly Christian, but to all authority and government in the world) "is ordained by God. Therefore he who resists it resists God's order, and those who resist it will incur judgment." Therefore, as Paul writes, a Christian cannot, under God and in good conscience, resist a government, the Turkish as little as the Roman, because he is speaking of authority that is everywhere.

The powerful are not to be feared by those who do good but by the wicked. For since the world does not fear God's coming judgment and does not avoid evildoing, therefore the present judicial authority of the government has been instituted that men may at least fear it and avoid judgment, since the world always sees only the present and is little concerned about what is coming on that Judgment Day.

The wicked rogues of this world say, "If God grants me borrowed time until the Judgment Day I still have a long time." Therefore they do not desist from evil deeds for fear of the coming judgment; but for fear of the present government and temporal condemnation they must put on a false and worldly piety.

"Would you have no fear of him who is in authority? Then do what is good, and you will receive his approval, for he is God's servant for your good. But if you do wrong, be afraid (Job 19:29), for he does not bear the sword in vain; he is the servant of God to execute his wrath on the wrongdoer. Therefore one must be subject" (note that he speaks simply of being subject, not of being lords, governors, mayors and rulers) "not only to avoid wrath but also for conscience' sake. For the same reason you also pay taxes" (that is, to their office) "on land and possessions, such as interest, taxes and tithes," because they cannot perform labor but must attend to their office (Rom. 13:3–6).

Just as God has ordained that the ministers of the Word and gospel in Christendom should be supported by the gospel and receive the dues for their office and service from the church, so God has also ordained that the worldly rulers receive their dues from their subjects so that they can be supported and carry out their office. "For they are God's servants attending to these things" (that is, preserving worldly peace and order). Otherwise no one would be safe from another, and if each took what belongs to someone else, no one could walk or travel through the country. Therefore in this respect they serve men for their good, those who believe as well as those with worldly piety, so that the wicked are made to fear and so become obedient and wear a bridle like a horse or mule, yes, a bit by which they are restrained (Ps. 32:9).

"So let each one of you give what you owe, taxes to whom taxes are due, revenue to whom revenue is due, and respect to whom respect is due" (Rom. 13:7). He says we should pay what we owe. But in anything that is contrary to God, faith and conscience (where God alone wants to dwell), God-fearing Christians do not owe anything. For he adds, "Respect to whom respect is due, honor to whom honor is due," that is, we should fear, reverence, and honor God above all in those things and keep ourselves unspotted from the world in whatever is against him (James 1:27). For Christ also says, "Give to everyone who begs from you" (Luke 6:30). He does not mean to give indiscriminately, or that I should give if someone should ask me for money to spend in loose living and gambling or to buy a gun, spear, or sword in order to kill or lay to ruin his enemy. Oh no! In this we are always to make and keep a Christian and godly distinction.

Even if I personally did not want to be an arsonist, yet paid someone else for that purpose; even if I – to be precise, myself – did not want to do something, yet paid someone else to do it, and then authorized that person to go; indeed, if I were an enemy of a magistrate or ruling lord, yet did not want to strangle him with my own hands, but instead equipped and sent someone else to carry out this deed; would I then not be punished as a murderer, as if I had carried out the deed myself? Indeed, most certainly I would, and with good reason! In this same manner, and even more so, God will bring punishment upon someone who personally does not shed blood, but allows others to fight in war in his or her stead, compensating and supporting them. These alternatives are one and the same, and before God merit the same reward.

57 "FOR WHAT HAVE I to do with judging outsiders?" says Paul (1 Cor. 5:12). This makes it clear once again that no disciple or follower of Christ may have dominion over the world and no Christian can be a ruler. But a ruler may indeed become a Christian if with Christ he lays aside his office, humbles himself, takes on Christ's mind, lays down his sword and takes up Christ's cross and follows him.

58 PAUL SAYS to the Corinthians: "To have lawsuits at all with one another means something lacking among you. Why not rather suffer wrong? But you yourselves wrong and defraud, and that, even your own brethren" (1 Cor. 6:7–8). From this it follows once more that no Christian may have or hold judicial office; law courts and suing at law are both done away with in the church of Christ.

59 PAUL DESCRIBES all the offices in the house of God and his church, how God appointed in the church first apostles, second prophets, third teachers, then workers of miracles, then healers, helpers, administrators, speakers in various kinds of tongues (1 Cor. 12:28; Eph. 4:11). But nowhere does he include the office of force, the sword, or the ruler; nowhere in the entire New Testament does one find that the apostles or Christians had executioners, police or imprisonment in the church, or employed them against anyone. Never did they go about in armor. For all of these things are not proper for Christians. When St. Peter converted a great crowd of about three thousand to the faith (Acts 2:41), where did he choose or appoint them a ruler to lord over them?

Therefore, if there had been – or were to have been in the future – rulers and force in Christ's house, the faithful apostle Paul would surely have described, established and announced it, as well as other offices, since he did not hold back anything from the church of Christ but proclaimed all of God's counsel (Acts 20:20).

60 PAUL SAYS TO THE CHURCH, "We are not lords over your faith, but we work with you for your joy" (2 Cor. 2:24). And Peter obligates the elders and admonishes them to "tend willingly the flock of God that is your charge, not for shameful gain but eagerly, not as domineering over those in your charge but by being examples to the flock" (1 Pet. 5:2).

61 "THE WEAPONS OF OUR WARFARE are not carnal," says Paul, "but spiritual" (2 Cor. 10:4). In other places he says the armor of God is the sword of the Spirit, namely, God's word, the breastplate of righteousness and love, the shield of faith, the helmet of salvation and hope (Eph. 6:14–17; 1 Thess. 5:8). That is the arsenal of armor for Christians and the weapons of the knights of Christ.

The weapons of earthly power and its knights are carnal and not spiritual; they are swords, spears, guns and halberds, they are javelins and clubs, they are murderous weapons of war to take lives. These two classes of weapons cannot exist together. Since they are essentially different, they cannot both be handled by one person. He who wants the one must leave the other.

No one can serve two masters at the same time. No one can travel on two roads at the same time. No one can set his foot down at more than one place. Here, too, the weapons of Christians and those of the world, the weapons of the Spirit and those of the flesh cannot be fused together.

Just as what is stated above cannot be done, neither can a Christian be a worldly ruler, or a worldly ruler a Christian. Christians do not fight in human fashion, says Paul (2 Cor. 10:3), but the world and its rulers wage war and fight solely in human fashion. Christians fight against the devil and sin and not against a human being; the world and its governments fight for honor and possessions against other lands and their peoples;

they daily let the devil and sin overcome them and take them prisoner. Christians contend for a heavenly inheritance and homeland, while worldly powers strive for an earthly inheritance and homeland. Christians fight for an imperishable heavenly crown, the absolute opposite of the other. Christians are a spectacle to the world, refuse to the world, and every man's outcast – they are fools for Christ's sake (1 Cor. 4:9–10); rulers rank high in the world, are illustrious and assured of honor, and consequently, since everyone lifts his hat, they go far wrong.

62 THE SWORD IS the absolute opposite of and contrary to true love (which is the first commandment in the church of Christ, the head and the summit of the Christian life). For the apostle Paul says, "Love is patient and kind" (1 Cor. 13:4). But the sword and its servants are quickly angered, abrupt and rough, short of temper like an enemy. Love is not envious, but the sword is not only envious, but returns evil for evil from that time on. Love is not resentful, is not puffed up; the sword and its servants clash with one another and puff themselves up with great power and might. Love does not seek its own gain, whereas the sword protects, seeks and preserves its own self-interest (Hos. 13; Rom. 13). Love is not easily provoked to anger, the sword is nothing but pure wrath, and a tool and instrument of wrath (Job 19:29). Love compels no one to do wrong, the sword is vengeance itself and repays every wrong with wrong (Rom. 13:4). Love endures all things, the sword endures nothing, but returns blow for blow. Paul says, "If I had everything and did not have love, I would gain nothing" (1 Cor. 13:17). Worldly authority, if it had everything but the sword, would be useless as governmental authority.

To sum up: Love has precedence among Christians, but in the world the sword has precedence;[9] therefore Christian love and the worldly sword cannot exist together, but the sword, and those who serve and wield it, are situated parallel to Christ's kingdom – outside his church and not in it. However, since it is still day, they may still enter in this manner: if they turn and become like children (Matt. 18:3).

63 PAUL WRITES TO TITUS, "Remind them to be submissive to rulers, obeying the government and ready for every good work" (note: "good work") (Titus 3:1). Thereby everything is excluded that is evil, contrary to the gospel, and against faith and conscience; he does not want us to be ready to do such things.

64 THE APOSTLE PETER TEACHES: "Be subject for the Lord's sake to every human institution, whether it be to the king as supreme, or to governors as sent by him to punish those who do wrong and to praise those who do right. For it is God's will that by doing right you should put to silence the ignorance of foolish men. Live as those who are free, yet without using your freedom as a pretext for evil" (1 Pet. 2:13–16). Thus they all teach submissiveness – but, however, as Peter himself

did: When he was forbidden to preach, and ordered to do wrong, he said, "We must obey God rather than men" (Acts 5:29).

Shadrach, Meshach, and Abednego did likewise (Dan. 3:16), and also Mattathias and his men. When a tyrannical power tried to force them to act contrary to the law of God, he said in a loud voice: "Even if all the nations that live under the rule of the king obey him, and have chosen to do his commandments, departing each one from the religion of his fathers, yet I and my sons and my brothers will live by the covenant of our fathers. Far be it from us to desert the law and the ordinances. We will not obey the king's words by turning aside from our religion to the right hand or to the left." (1 Macc. 2:19–22).

That is what the ancients did, that is what Peter did; yes, no Christian has ever permitted himself to be forced to do anything contrary to God and the faith. That is why from the beginning Christians have suffered so much torture, pain and death at the hands of emperors and rulers. Therefore, in whatever is right and Christian, to that extent we should also show submission. It never occurred to the apostles to teach anything more than that.

65 TO THE THESSALONIANS Paul writes: "The Lord will slay the Antichrist with the breath of his mouth and destroy him by the radiance of his coming" (2 Thess. 2:8). He does not say with soldiers and weapons.

66 THE LORD CHRIST REVEALED himself to the holy Apostle John with a two-edged sword issuing from his mouth[10] (Rev. 1:16; 19:15). From this we, his disciples and believers, learn that the sword does not belong in our hands but in our mouth – that is, the sword of the Spirit, God's word (Heb. 4:12; Eph. 6:17) – and that we should not bear or use the bloody sword.

67 THE TWENTY-FOUR ELDERS in the Revelation of John who appear around the throne of God cast their crowns before the throne. Where, then, will those be who, here and now, refuse to cast away their crowns but instead want to be crowned and honored by all men, and for the sake of their temporal crowns, tear and bite at each other so that blood flows? They will not be among the elders gathered around the throne of God, but around Lucifer's throne. The elders say, "You are worthy, our Lord and God, to receive glory and honor and power, for you created all things" (Rev. 4:10–11). But these people regard themselves worthy of receiving and accepting glory and honor and great reverence, which a Christian can neither accept nor take to himself.

68 "IF ANYONE HAS AN EAR, let him hear. He that leads into captivity shall go into captivity; he that kills with the sword must be killed with the sword. This calls for the patience and the faith of the saints" (Rev. 13:9–10). It is as though he wanted to say, only with this will they overcome. For with patience Christians overcome all their foes. Patience is a weapon for every conflict. John says, "Our faith is the victory that overcomes the world" (1 John 5:4). Therefore Christ teaches his followers in the gospel, "Possess your souls with patience" (Luke 21:19); nowhere does he teach them to possess their souls with swords and spears like the tribes of Iscariots and Pharisees, and the soldiers on the Mount of Olives who seized Jesus and imprisoned him (Matt. 26).

That is why they had to be imprisoned in Vespasian's prisons[11] and lose their lives by the sword of the Romans. And that would be a small matter if only they did not also have to come before God's judgment on Judgment Day. For they will have to appear there and be cast into the prison of outermost darkness where there is eternal weeping and wailing and gnashing of teeth (Matt. 13:42, 50; 25:30). At this judgment they will first be judged by the two-edged sword of the Son of God (Rev. 1:16; 19:15) when he says to them: "Depart from me, you cursed, into the eternal fire prepared for the devil and his angels" (Matt. 25:41).

This will be the lot of all who even today put the members of Christ into prison and kill them because of their faith under the name of heretics. This they will do, says Christ, because they have not known me nor my Father (John 16:3; 1 Cor. 2:8; 1 John 3:1), as if he were saying: therefore they will not know you either.

69 ANYONE WHO SAYS a Christian can be in the government, which defends the wicked, destroys devout true believers (for that is what takes place), kills the innocent Jesus as a revolutionary and sets Barabbas, who committed murder in the revolt, free; and promotes savage horror and kills the friends of God while boasting of being the servants and slaves of God, but does not want to see or listen to the Son of God or his people; such a person strays far away from the truth.

Likewise: Christ, the Lord, tells John in his Revelation that in the place and realm where Christians (true Christians) and God's faithful witnesses are put to death for their faith, there is the devil's throne and dwelling place (Rev. 2:9–10). The tyrants and murderers of the devout ought to hang this inscription around their necks and write it on their helmets and thrones. Otherwise the Lord himself will do it, so that they will not be able to blot it out unless they repent and become new men.

Pilate could be considered holy, Herod pious and honorable, if one compares their deeds with those of the princes, who boastfully call themselves Christian and evangelical. To be sure, Herod and Pilate (who after all did not boast of Christ and his faith) killed Christ, who was leading four, five, or seven thousand people about in the desert and teaching them (Matt. 14:21; 15:38; John 6:10). They tolerated him a long time, and finally, as though under compulsion, they put him to death.

But these, who boast of having Christ and his truth, whenever they can find a single true Christian who leads only two or three people out of their ungodly lives and their adulterated church, such a person they put to death thirstily, and cannot tolerate him. How can they then be Christians? Much to the contrary: consider the sins, vices and great blasphemy and desecration the powerful enact against God, which they shower upon the acts of God and Christ to such a degree that the very elements pale and tremble – even Pilate and Herod did not do such! – not to speak of their exorbitant pomp and presumption. Alas, what Christianity this is! Whoever is able should sweat blood and weep over such Christians. And boast as they may, their deeds are in plain view, so they cannot deny them; from this it follows once more – and doubly so – that they cannot be Christians. It would be a fact: If taking usury, snatching everything for themselves, violating girls and married women, fornicating without shame, creating widows and orphans, drinking up and laying to ruin the countryside and its inhabitants were Christian and evangelical, they would be the greatest multitude and their warriors the best Christians.

70 CHRISTIANS AND THE WORLD are as different as heaven and earth. The world is world and remains world and acts like the world, and all the world is one world. The Christian, however, is called out of the world and is required no longer to conform to the world (John 15:19; 2 Cor. 6:14–18; Rev. 18:4; Rom. 12:2), no longer to be its consort (Eph. 5:6–7), no longer to walk in its disorderly confusion (1 Pet. 4:1–6), no longer to pull its yoke (2 Cor. 6:14–18).

Worldlings live according to the flesh, which rules them. They believe no one is around to observe; therefore they need the sword in their realm. Christians live according to the Spirit, which rules them. They believe the Lord is watching, that he is attentive; therefore they do not need the sword among themselves.

The Christians' victory is "the faith which overcomes the world" (1 John 5:4). The world's victory is the sword with which it conquers.

To Christians is given an inner joy; they have joy in their hearts, holding to the unity in the Spirit through the bond of peace (John 14:15–27; Eph. 4:3). The world has no peace; by sword and coercion alone it attempts to keep outward peace.

The Christian has patience, as the apostle writes: "Since therefore Christ suffered, . . . arm yourselves likewise with the same mind" (1 Pet. 4:1). The world arms itself for the sake of revenge; it fights.

The Christian who can suffer everything for the sake of God is the most honorable. The world considers most dutiful the one who can defend himself with the sword against everyone else.

To sum up: Friendship with the world is enmity[12] with God (James 4:4), and whoever desires to be a friend of the world makes himself an enemy of God.

If being a Christian could be accomplished with words and an empty name, if Christendom could regulate itself as it desired, if Christ would take pleasure in what pleases them, and the cross itself were to be sustained by means of the ugly sword, then rulers and subjects, indeed, most of the world, would probably be Christians. However, since man must be born anew (John 3:7), must die to his old life in baptism (Rom. 6:3–4), and with Christ arise to a new life and Christian walk, that cannot be the case. It is easier for a camel to go through the eye of a needle than for a rich man (specifically, those who are rulers over others) to enter into the kingdom of God or into true Christianity (Matt. 19:24).

ARGUMENTS OF THE WORLD

71 *So says the world: The words of Christ, "the rulers of the Gentiles lord it over them and their great men exercise coercion, but it shall not be so among you" (Matt. 20:25; Mark 10:42; Luke 22:25), refer only to the apostles, and do not include the church as a whole.*

ANSWER: This was spoken not only to the twelve but to all the churches and members of Christ in general. It does not say, It shall not be so among you twelve, but just as Christ did not domineer, so we also should not domineer but follow after him in cross-bearing and suffering.

Here, in peace there is no cutting to bits; but through the cutting sword, peace is cut up. Isaiah the prophet says that Christ will bear the government upon his shoulders (Isa. 9:6), and not possess or defend it with the sword, but maintain it by teaching. Likewise, the Apostle says, "We are oppressed" (1 Cor. 4:9 ff); and "Christ is given as a sign that will be opposed" (Luke 2:34). Also: "If they persecute me, they will persecute you" (John 15:20). "If they have called the householder Beelzebub, how much more will they do so to those of his household" (Matt. 10:25).

Being addressed as "gracious lord" and as "Beelzebub" are two very different things. All of this is now common knowledge, that no Christian can be a "gracious lord" or a ruler, or be so addressed by the world, nor will the rulers be Christians.

72 *They say: "But after all, the apostles carried swords. For when Christ was about to be seized Peter drew his sword and cut off the High Priest's servant's ear" (Matt. 26:51).*

ANSWER: It was like this: At that time Peter had a sword because they had just killed and eaten the Paschal lamb according to Jewish custom; and he took it because he had clearly understood from the Lord that he would on that very night be betrayed and taken. For the disciples were still clinging to much Jewishness. It does not follow, however, that we are to do the same.

Nor does it say that all of them had swords. They at that time still observed the Passover, but that does not mean that we should also keep it. Christ celebrated the Jewish Passover with them so that he might fulfill it, and instituted the Lord's Supper to be held henceforth.

That is why it happened that Peter still wanted to fight with the sword: so that Christ would reject it when he rebuked him, "Put your sword back into its place, for all who take the sword will perish by the sword" (Matt. 26:52). With these words he absolutely cuts off the use of the sword and requires of his people (among whom there is no place for the sword, as he plainly says) that they put it down. And Peter then put it into its place and left it there.

Consequently one finds nowhere that the other disciples ever again produced or drew a sword. Hence we should not pull out a sword in Christ's church, for the worldly sword and the spiritual sword cannot dwell together in one sheath; each has its own sheath. The spiritual one belongs to the church of Christ, the worldly one to the world among the wicked, who strike with it.

That is why he announced to them that evil and punishment are attached to it; that whoever fights with the sword will be vanquished by it. For like a madman one will thereby have drawn the sword upon himself. The instrument with which one conducts his affairs will be the instrument of his reward or punishment; one sword whets the other (Prov. 27:17), one rascal punishes the other, and thus they remove peace from the world (Rev. 6:4).

Therefore, what the immature disciples did in ignorance – for which Christ rebuked them and gave them a command – took place as an example for us, that we should not do so. For Christians are to fight with the cross and overcome with the cross, never wiping out or repaying insolence with insolence or audacity with audacity.

For the man who comes sword in hand does not have good intentions, and it is the first signal for seeking refuge. Therefore Christians cannot be servants or bearers of the sword, nor assert power or wage war with it, because they have committed themselves to the one who taught peace. Peter also denied his Lord (Matt. 26:69); would you therefore say, "Peter did it," and thereby claim that it is right to deny Christ? Oh, no! Thus likewise for using the sword, for which he was rebuked.

73 *They say: When the Lord answered Peter, "All who take the sword will perish by the sword" (Matt. 26:52), he meant that those who draw the sword on their own authority, and not according to its proper use, will be slain by the sword. Also that the words in Matthew 5:39, "You shall not resist evil or kill," do not refer to the government, but only to the individual. In the same way it says, "Thou shalt not kill" (Exod. 20:13 and elsewhere), yet on the other hand there were many laws on how to deal with this or that evildoer in order to eradicate evil. Hence, they say, there can be a ruler among Christian people.*

ANSWER: They are trying to make these passages refer to special persons and deny their validity for worldly government, but it is obvious that Christ applied and cited this statement just as it was given to judges and rulers in the Old Testament (for among the ancients no one could have carried out such commands on his own but this had to take place through those officially appointed) – since Jesus used not the singular "you," but the plural "you" which excludes no Christian[13] when he said "You shall not resist evil."

It therefore follows that such passages do not refer to particular individuals but apply to all Christians in general, that none of them is to fight with the sword or resist evil. When Peter struck out with his sword, Jesus told him to let them proceed (Matt. 26:51–54), as if he wanted to say, "Just let them exercise their evil intentions, in so far as is permitted them. The deed has its judge, so we are not to avenge ourselves." That is the obligation of Christians in every age in adversity and tribulation. We do not oppose worldly authority instituted by God, but acknowledge that it is necessary in the world. We also commit ourselves to obeying them in outward matters in so far as this is right. But we do not transfer the dictates of the law to the New Testament.

In Leviticus we read that anyone who is convicted of adultery on the testimony of two or three witnesses shall be stoned to death without mercy (Lev. 20:10; Deut. 17:6; Heb. 10:28). Now if they want to transfer the government of the Old Testament to the New, they cannot ban the adulterer for his betterment as Paul teaches, but must judge him according to the severity of the old law. If they are unwilling to judge in accord with the Old and New Testaments they must judge in accord with the imperial laws like the heathen. So they act neither according to the Old, nor to the New Testament.

74 *They say: After all, Christ laid hands on and drove the buyers and sellers out of the temple with a scourge (John 2:15).*

ANSWER: This was still his prerogative, for the law was not yet annulled, and the New Testament had not yet been separated from the Old or confirmed by his death.

For a testament is not valid, in force, or confirmed until the death of the one who made it (Heb. 9:17). Then when that has taken place it is obligatory to follow it completely in every detail. But just as it is not true that a scourge is in itself a sword, it is also untrue and much more so, that Christ thereby wanted Christians to apply or use human coercion against anyone.

75 *They say: How is it then that the law and the gospel do not contradict one another, and that the law is not annulled by faith and is not supposed to be against those who live in the Spirit, and yet the law and the gospel are not to be practiced together essentially by one person?*

ANSWER: The function of the law and the office of Christ are widely different. For if the function of the law and the office of Christ were intended to be a single office or practiced together, then Christ would have done wrong in forbidding his disciples to take vengeance when they referred to Elijah (Luke 9:54–55).

But the outward shadowy and servile law in the Old Testament that was laid upon former times, whether in reference to the priesthood or the office of judgment, and the law concerning force having dominion over the nations or repaying and punishing evil with evil as was their practice, was only an outward foreshadowing of what is inward and spiritual. It was not given to be valid and to stand forever in its former outward expression but to be valid only until an age of a better law. For "if there is a change in the priesthood, there is necessarily a change in the law as well" (Heb. 7:12). If the first had been faultless or sufficient, it would not have been necessary to seek a second (Heb. 8:7). But they were made aware of something lacking. Thus the age in which the outward and carnal law was given, in so far as its preparatory purpose and meaning are concerned, has not been supplanted, but fulfilled and completed in Christ (Matt. 5:17).

Thus the outward law (which pointed to the inward and spiritual law and is no longer valid in the older sense) accomplished this – that Christ is the end of the law. (Rom. 10:4). For when he annulled the first and servile law he established the other which is spiritual and makes known what the outward and servile law prefigured and represented (Heb. 10:9), and he perfects and fulfills it and says that not one iota will pass from the law until all has been accomplished and fulfilled (Matt. 5:18), and that he did not come to destroy but to fulfill.

Since the outward law did not last beyond the coming of the new and spiritual, which completes and fulfills the old and outward law (in its meaning), it follows that the two cannot be in opposition. Yet they cannot both be practiced together essentially or enforced as if they were the same. But Christ has made the two into one. He has broken down the middle wall and brought everything together, so that there is neither Jew nor Greek, but a new creation (Eph. 2:14–15), and all is under the New Testament, so that people are no longer followers of Moses or heathen but they are Christians (Gal. 3:28; 6:15).

Therefore, as the Levitical priesthood and the judgmental law to punish the transgressor were given through Moses to be practiced together, so also Christ has inaugurated the royal priesthood (1 Pet. 2:9) and also the royal law, which is spiritual and not carnal, for his followers, the Christians (James 2:8), to be practiced together in the Christian church, punishing transgression with exclusion (Matt. 18:17).

76 *They also say: The Son is never in conflict with the Father. He therefore does not break what the Father has once ordained, nor do away with it. So if the Father has ordained government it must also remain in Christ, or the Son would be in conflict with the Father.*

ANSWER: It is true that the Son is not in conflict with the Father; the two are one (John 17:22). But it does not follow that what the Father had once established must remain in Christ. For then Christ's grace would be in vain. The reason is that, after the fall, the Father condemned all men to death. But by his death Christ removed the might and power of death and has thus restored life in all who believe in his Name. He is therefore not in conflict with the Father but has instead fulfilled the Father's promise. Furthermore, God ordained and commanded circumcision so firmly to Abraham that any uncircumcised male infant was to be cut off from the nation (Gen. 17:14). But in Christ it is abolished. Also, the Father commanded that they love their friend and hate their enemy (Matt. 5:43); when Saul did not do this, but spared the enemy, the king of the Amalekites, and let him live, he was expelled from the kingdom.

Nevertheless, Christ commands that we love not only our friends but also our enemies. There are many other things that the Father ordained, such as sacrifices, the Sabbath and the like which have ceased and ended in Christ (in whom the essence is the same). Therefore one should not say so arrogantly that the Son is for that reason in conflict with the Father, but rather: What the Father has ordained in Christ will remain in him and will not be changed – such as love, peace, unity and community. But what he has ordained outside of Christ, such as death, wrath, ruthlessness, cursing, swearing, revenge and their servants will also be out of place in Christendom.

77 *They may also say: We find that the prophets prophesied about Christ. Yet they do not expel government from the institution of worship and service to God, but instead show what its office and service in Christ is really to be. As Isaiah says, "Kings shall be your foster fathers, and their queens your nursing mothers" (Isa. 49:23). Likewise in the Revelation of John: "The kings of the earth shall bring their glory and honor" into the New Jerusalem (Rev. 21:24).*

ANSWER: We believe that where the prophets foretell and predict about Christ they reject nobody from the testament of God's grace, because Christ is an open door into eternal life for all mankind. But the ruler under Christ must rid himself of his domination and worldly reign because it does not befit a Christian to rule, but to be subject (John 6:15; Matt. 20:25). Rulers must arm themselves with the mind of Christ, who suffered and bore the cross here on earth (1 Pet. 4:1; Luke 9:23). They must also become children of his Spirit. They must pass through the eye of the needle (Matt. 19:24), enter through the narrow gate (Matt. 7:13) which will brush the sword from their side. They must turn around and become like children if they are to become Christians (Matt. 18:3).

For the prophet Isaiah, when he says, kings shall become the foster fathers of the church of Christ, adds: "With their faces to the ground they shall bow down to you and lick the dust from your feet" (Isa. 49:23). Elsewhere he says that every mountain and hill shall be lowered and made level with the valleys of the earth (Isa. 40:4). That means giving up domination and power and splendor, becoming lowly, amending one's life and turning around; it means conversion. And it shows, by virtue of the new nature in the Spirit (Rom. 7:6), that they will truly serve God and his church as Paul did, who was such a man. Paul says: "We were gentle among you, like a nurse taking care of her children. So, being affectionately desirous of you, we were ready to share with you not only the gospel of God but also our own lives" (1 Thess. 2:7–8).

Oh, I wish to God there were many such foster fathers and kings on earth who are made such kings and priests of God through the blood of Christ (Rev. 1:6). They would bring all their glory and honor, their crowns and fame into the New Jerusalem (2 Cor. 1; 1 Thess. 2). Here there is no mention of worldly kings and rulers of the world, for those who wield the sword and act violently and rudely are not foster fathers, but servants of vengeance among the ungodly of this world. And if they were supposed to bring their glory and honor, and dominion, pomp and pride into the New Jerusalem, then Lucifer would not have fallen but would well have been permitted to stay in heaven.

78 *The world says further: But we read expressly that when the soldiers came to John the Baptist and asked what they should do, he did not forbid warfare, but said, "Do no violence or injustice to anyone, and be content with your wages" (Luke 3:14).*

ANSWER: The law was not yet abrogated or brought to perfection. The curtain in the temple was not yet rent, and the New Testament not yet differentiated from the Old. John was simply a forerunner of the paths of Christ to make an opening and beginning in Israel (Matt. 3:3). But Christ came to us from the Father fully prepared as a new and living path (Heb. 10:20); he says then, since he came later, "It was said to the men of old, 'You shall not kill (Exod. 20:13; 21), but I say to you, he who is angry with his brother shall be liable to the judgment; whoever insults his brother shall be liable to the council, and whoever says, 'You fool!' shall be liable to the hell of fire" (Matt. 5:21–22) – not to mention him who kills. Likewise: "You have heard that it was said, 'An eye for an eye, a tooth for a tooth, a hand for a hand' (Exod. 20:13; 21:24; Deut. 19:21). But I say to you, do not resist one who is evil. But if anyone strikes you on the right cheek, turn to him the other also" (Matt. 5:39).

Where, then, is there a place for a soldier in Christendom? There no soldier will or can stay, for the gospel removes his sword; the combatant and defender with a sword has no place there. For the wolf must become a sheep and lay aside his wolfish fangs. The lion must eat grass like cattle. They shall graze together in one herd (Isa. 11:6; 65:25). For Christ and the apostles teach their followers: Love your enemies, do good to those who hate you (Matt. 5:44). The Apostle Paul teaches: "Beloved, never avenge yourselves." Likewise, "If your enemy is hungry, feed him; if he is thirsty, give him drink" (Rom. 12:19–20). The Apostle Peter writes to the brethren: "Do not return evil for evil or reviling for reviling; but on the contrary bless, for to this you have been called, that you may obtain a blessing" (1 Pet. 3:9).

All of this and much more abolishes wars and soldiers in Christianity. Thus there remains a great difference between John and Christ. John baptized only with water unto penitence and repentance; but Christ, with the Holy Spirit and with fire. If we were to follow John the Baptist we would still have to observe the Jewish Passover and many other things, for he did not institute the Lord's Supper; only Christ did. But God wanted them with their soldiers to follow John the Baptist and be content with their wages. How much pillage would then have been avoided! And if they did no violence or injustice to anyone, they would soon discontinue warfare, for wars and the deeds of warfare are nothing but violence and injustice.

79 *In their blindness they say: After all, Christ said to his disciples: "Let him who has a purse take it, and likewise a bag. And let him who has nothing sell his mantle and buy a sword" (Luke 22:36).*

ANSWER: Yes, my friend, but not an outward one, not a bloody sword meant for striking. Otherwise Paul would not have spoken truly when he said: "We are not carrying on a worldly war, for the weapons of our warfare are not worldly" (Eph. 6:12; 2 Cor. 10:3–4). Christ also says, if your hand or your foot cause you to sin, cut them off (Matt. 5:30). But he does not mean that they should be cut off with the sword. Likewise the words "buy a sword" are not to be taken literally but understood spiritually. For if he had referred to the outward bloody sword, it would not have been necessary for Christ to command it, for there is a natural inclination in man to use it. Jews, heathen, and Turks have swords; God has no pleasure in them.

Therefore Christ neither meant nor wanted that. Christ is here depicting for them the difficulties to come and the conflict against sin and ungodliness in the world into which he is about to send them, so that they would prepare themselves with the sword of the Spirit, with the Christian sword, which is the Word of God (Eph. 6:17). That is why Christ adds, "For I tell you that this scripture must be fulfilled in me, 'And he was reckoned with transgressors'" (Luke 22:37), as if he were telling them: This will also be your lot; therefore equip yourselves with the armor of the Spirit. And it is clearly shown that he really did not mean the bloody sword by his response to the disciples, "It is enough" (Luke 22:38), when they said, "Lord, here are two swords." That is to say, from now on it is not a matter of fighting with the sword, but of suffering for the sake of the gospel and bearing the cross.

Therefore it is now necessary to grasp the spiritual sword, the Word of God. If Christ had been speaking of buying the outward sword he would not have said that two were enough, for there were twelve of them, and more besides, and their number was increasing daily, and two swords would not have been enough. For each to have had one would have necessitated everyone selling his mantle.

And if Christ hereby meant that they should carry and use a sword, they did not carry out his wishes very well. For one finds nowhere that they used the sword to defend themselves or the gospel against their enemies, and when Peter used it, the Lord rebuked him, saying that he was not to fight with the sword but should sheath it (Matt. 26:52). Otherwise Christ would have contradicted himself, for he always said, "If anyone strikes you on the right cheek, turn to him the other also" (Matt. 5:39), and "Do not resist one who is evil." The apostles must then also have been against Christ when they forbade taking revenge (Rom. 12:19), or repaying evil for evil, or reviling for reviling (1 Pet. 3:9), not to mention blow for blow. The prophets would also have had to be against Christ when they prophesied how in the last times the peoples of the church of Christ would melt their swords into hoes and their lances into pruning hooks, scythes and saws, and would not use weapons against one another (Isa. 2:4; Mic. 4:3).

All of this and much more would be wrong and in vain if Christ had ordered them to buy outward swords. That is not the case and he is referring to no other sword than the one he himself had, namely, the two-edged sword that proceeds from his mouth (Rev. 1:16; 19:15; Heb. 4:12). With this sword he now wants his disciples to arm themselves because he is about to be taken from them through suffering. For it would indeed be needed by every one of them.

Therefore we should be satisfied with two swords – the sword of government which is and must be in the world, and the sword of the Spirit and Word of God, which is the only one in the church of Christ. For when there is enough and more is added, that is too much and therefore comes from evil (Matt. 5:37). Or the two swords can be understood to mean the Word of God – the divine teaching – as it is contained in the Scriptures of the Old and New Testaments, which can also be interpreted as two swords. Since they come from one Spirit, we are to be armed with both of them.

80 *Then, if they raise the objection: the government is ordained by God (Rom. 13:1) to explore zealously what is right and good according to God's word, and by means of their office as rulers to eradicate false worship and compel and hold their subjects and churches to true worship.*

ANSWER: There is not a single word from the apostles or Christ saying that Christians and God's children are to be held and driven to church services with the sword. For they have not received a slavish spirit (Rom. 8:15), but the Holy Spirit testifies through David about Christ's people, saying, "Your people will offer themselves freely on the day of your might" (Ps. 110:3).

Therefore those who use the sword to assist their churches forsake God and are not servants of Christ; they rob God of what is his and give it over to human might. Yes, those who dare to force and compel people into their churches, forcing them with the citizen's sword, compulsion, oppression, prison, tower confinement, fire and water, are swine herders who need to have clubs and are not shepherds of Christ's sheep who know their Shepherd's voice and follow of their own accord (John 10:16). Yes, they are a slavish church, bound to the letter, and not of the Spirit of God and Christ (Rom. 7:6).

For "cursed are they who trust in man and make flesh their arm," says the prophet, "whose heart turns away from God and who put their trust in princes and in the children of men, in whom there is no help" (Jer. 17:5; Ps. 146:3; 117:8). Let them hear what God says about this through the prophet: "Woe to those who dare to rule my people with violence and force" (Ezek. 34:4). Therefore let those, who snatch the ark of the Lord with violence and want to have it for themselves, see to it that they do not fare like the Philistines who had to return it in disgrace (1 Sam. 4).

81 *They say: In the parable of the feast Christ told them to "compel people to come in" (Luke 14:23).*[14]

ANSWER: But this in no way means with the sword, force, war and captivity, but by the Word of God they must be compelled in heart and conscience to enter his church and be called forth from the highways and the hedges of their wrong path of life, teaching and hope behind which they are hiding – as the Samaritan woman was also compelled to believe when Christ told her what she had done (John 4:29). Likewise Apollos constantly confuted the Jews, showing by the Scriptures that Jesus was the Christ (Acts 18:28).

Christ desires no other compulsion. It is the devil who compels and forces people into his realm with executioners and police, prison, suffering and torture, with sword and club. But Christ wants a voluntary heart (2 Cor. 6:1–12; Phil. 1:28), for when the disciples of John came to him, he did not command them to seize people and force them to believe but to bring them to faith through preaching and miracles (Matt. 11). He did not demand that they seize the rich young man, who watched sadly and then went away (Matt. 19:22), and compel him to become a disciple.

Also, when Jesus came into his home country and the people refused to believe him, he did not compel them to believe, nor did he perform many signs because of their unbelief (Matt. 13:54–58). When many of his disciples left him, he did not force them to stay but said to the others, "Will you also go away" (John 6:66)? He did not want to hold them through force, for if they had stayed reluctantly it would have amounted to the same as if they had gone away. Likewise, when his disciples said, "Do you know that the Pharisees were offended by you?" he answered, "Let them alone, they are blind leaders of the blind" (Matt. 15:12, 14).

Christ says, "No one can come to me unless the Father who sent me draws him" (not the sword) (John 6:44). For the sword can neither give nor take away faith; it is a gift of God (Eph. 2:8). It is God who is at work in you, both to will and to do (Phil. 2:13). Those whom the Spirit of God impels are his children (Rom. 8:14); not those who are impelled by prison, tower confinement, suffering and torture. Therefore the prophet says: O Lord, you know that I am leading the flock in your ways; I have not forced them, for I have never desired the death of any man (Jer. 17:16).[15]

82 *Now they say: Paul always writes clearly that rulers are ordained by God and are the servants of God (Rom. 13:1). Why then can they not be Christians in that office?*

ANSWER: If having the name of ruler made one a Christian, then the Roman tyrants, the emperors Claudius and Nero must also have been Christians, because Paul calls them, scepters and all, servants of God (Rom. 13:6). For it is certain that Paul wrote this from Corinth to the brethren in Rome, where these heathen tyrants reigned, and Paul is speaking of powers that exist everywhere and calls them God's servants.

Thus the Turk is also such a servant of God and would have to be a Christian if the name made the Christian. But that is not at all the meaning. For the Lord calls Nebuchadnezzar his servant (Jer. 43:10), and he calls King Cyrus and the king of Assyria a rod of his anger (Isa. 10:5). Likewise Christ in his prophecy against the Jews calls the Roman emperors Titus and Vespasian, with their hosts, God's army, his instrument, his servants, even though they were mere heathen (Matt. 22:21).

Therefore, just as there are two kinds of angels, good and bad, as one finds in Scripture, which calls both kinds angels (Ps. 78:49), so God also has two kinds of servants on earth. For in the great house of this world there are not only gold and silver vessels, but also wood and clay, some for honorable and some for ignoble use (2 Tim. 2:20), namely, the vessels of wrath, that is, servants of vengeance who punish with death and the sword, who are prepared for damnation; and vessels of mercy (that is, servants who discipline with the ban for correction in order to acquire grace again) (Rom. 9:21–23): those he has prepared for glory, whom he has called, namely us, out of all nations (1 Thess. 5:9).

83 *Then they say: Since the wicked man who sits in the place of authority is God's servant, then the believer who trusts in God can govern better than the godless heathen; for we have an explicit word, they say, that a Christian can be a ruler: Even in the time of Paul, Christians were in places of authority, for he wrote to his own people and their* *masters how they should relate to one another (Col. 3:22; 1 Pet. 2:13–14). Similarly he wrote to Timothy that believers who had masters should not despise them, for they were brethren (1 Tim. 6:1–2). And since the apostles permitted (they say) a man to be a master – indeed, even to have slaves, which is harsh and unfitting, whether there are one, two, or many – and yet remain a Christian, Christians can be rulers among us today.*

ANSWER: Paul's writing about slaves can only mean that they were house servants – slaves bought with money (Exod. 21). Peter and Paul do not call them anything else. They admonish them not to resist serfdom, but to obey their owners. For it would not be proper, since they were purchased, not to perform that for which they were purchased. From all this it can be concluded, from both the Old and the New Testaments, that the apostles were speaking only of purchased slaves, admonishing them to do their work. It does not say that they were speaking of government, as the false ones claim.

84 *Then they assert that Nicodemus and Joseph of Arimathea were both councilors and rulers in Jerusalem, but nevertheless, secret disciples of Christ: devout, God-fearing men, of whom Scripture testifies (Matt. 27:57). Likewise, Erastus was a city treasurer, but nevertheless a Christian, they say (Rom. 16:23). When Philip brought the eunuch of the Queen of Ethiopia to faith and baptized him, he let him remain in power and office (Acts 8). Likewise Cornelius (Acts 10:1), Sergius Paulus the magistrate (Acts 13:7), and*

the centurion whose servant Christ healed (Matt. 8:13) were also believers and did not leave their office, they say. Matthew also remained in his position at customs after his conversion until he was chosen as an apostle (Matt. 9:9; Luke 5:27).

ANSWER: It is true, as they say, that these men came to faith, and this we grant. But when they say that they remained in government, those are their own empty words, and it is up to them to prove them with Scripture and to show that Christ commanded the sword in his church and that a person is a member of Christ even if he bears a sword.

For we do not read that Erastus remained a collector of revenue, but that he was Paul's traveling companion, for in Acts nineteen he sent him to serve in Macedonia (Acts 19:22). Likewise Manaen, a member of the court of Herod the Tetrarch, was in the church at Antioch, where they assembled a whole year (Acts 11:26; 13:1). It does not say, "at Herod's court or in the government." To the Philippians Paul writes: "All the saints greet you, especially those of Caesar's household" (Phil. 4:22). He does not say that they were still at Caesar's court or in his house. We read, to be sure, of others who are similar. Thus Paul, who had the great power and authority of the High Priests (Acts 9:14; 26:10), did not retain it when he was baptized and became a brother.

In summary, the apostles and Paul simply preached the gospel to the eunuch of Ethiopia, to Cornelius, to Sergius Paulus and all the rest: "Worldly princes rule the nations, but it shall not be so with you. The mighty are called 'your lordship' but it shall not be so among you" (Matt. 20:25; Luke 22:25). Likewise, "Unless you change and become like children" (Matt. 18:3), without domineering, without exaltation, you will not enter into God's kingdom. Likewise, "Judge not that you be not judged" (Matt. 7:1). Likewise, "If any man would come after me, let him deny himself and take up his cross and follow me" (note: the cross) (Matt. 16:24). Again, "Put your sword back in its place" for it is no longer right to fight with it (Matt. 26:52). Likewise, that the Lord became angry with the man who, because of a debt, took his fellow servant by the throat and threw him into prison (Matt. 18:34).

The disciples of Christ were themselves to know and consider what manner of spirit they were of and not, like Elijah, want to call down fire from heaven or destroy anyone in revenge (Luke 9:54–55). Likewise, that Christ escaped when the people wanted to make him their ruler and king (John 6:15), that he refused to judge or divide the inheritance (Luke 12:14), that he refused to condemn to death the woman taken in adultery, although the law demanded that she be put to death (John 8:11); that Christ says his kingdom is not of this world and his servants do not stand armed with sword and spear (John 18:36); and that those whom God called and foreknew he also charged to be conformed to the image of his Son (Rom. 8:29). Likewise, that they would be taken before kings and princes and rulers and before their councils for the sake of Christ's name and be tortured (Matt. 10:18). He does not say that they, the Christians, will themselves be governors and councilors. And when the disciples said, "Here are two swords," he answered, "It is enough" (Luke 22:38).

Indeed, the apostles proclaimed the teaching that they should no longer be conformed to this world (Rom. 12:2), that they should be subject to the authorities (and are not to be rulers) (Rom. 13:1; 1 Pet. 2:13). "What have I to do with judging outsiders," says Paul (1 Cor. 5:12). And: "Something is lacking among you that you sue one another at law. Why do you not rather suffer wrong?" (1 Cor. 6:7) And: "Though we live in the world, we do not fight as men fight, for the weapons of our warfare are not carnal but spiritual" (2 Cor. 10:3–4), but we are to "fight the good fight, having faith and a good conscience" (1 Tim. 1:18). He also said "Put on the breastplate of righteousness. As shoes for your feet put on whatever will make you ready to proclaim the gospel of peace. In all circumstances take the shield of faith, . . . the helmet of salvation and the sword of the Spirit, which is the word of God" (Eph. 6:14–17). And Peter: "Since therefore Christ suffered in the flesh, arm yourselves also with the same intention" (1 Pet. 4:1). Likewise in Revelation, "He who puts men into prison will himself be imprisoned, and he who kills with the sword will be slain by it" (Rev. 13:10).

From all this and from many other Scriptures – as the Apostle says, "only, live your life in a manner worthy of the gospel of Christ" (Phil. 1:27) – they could well have learned that they could never be worldly princes, lords, magistrates, governors, judges, or army captains if they wanted to be followers of Christ. Neither Paul nor any other apostles of Christ bore a worldly office of judgment or a sword. He says to his entire brotherhood, "Follow me, taking me as your example" (Phil. 3:17). They preached no other or different gospel than what they themselves had accepted and received from Christ.

85 *They may also say, Governors are rulers and together they compose the government (1 Cor. 12:28), along with: "if someone governs, let him do it with care" (Rom. 12:8) – saying, that this is addressed to governing authorities.*

ANSWER: But that is not the case. For then the Scriptures would give more evidence that at the time of the apostles there was such a worldly government in their church. But there is none, and all the Scriptures speak against it. For Christ did not entrust any outward rule to his church, but an inner rule which shall be governed by the Word of truth. And consequently, concerning the assignment of the people for outward tasks, and work and service to the poor, managers and stewards in the church of Christ were appointed to manage and care for temporal needs (Acts 6:1–6). But this is not government with the sword.

86 *The world says, and may well raise the objection: The prophet also says the opposite, "Beat your plowshares into swords, and your pruning hooks into spears, and your pruning knives, scythes, and saws into lances" (Joel 3:10).*

ANSWER: The prophet said this about his own age; for it was in the Old Testament that they marched against their enemies with swords, spears and javelins, for they were commanded to hate their enemies and they were often sent by God's command to wipe out their enemies. But now, in the New Testament, it is not so, but is forbidden by Christ. Therefore a distinction must be made between the figurative and the actual, the carnal and the spiritual, the law and grace or truth, between Moses and Christ, yes, between the Old and New Testament, Judaism and Christianity.

Otherwise we would be half Jews, half Christians and who knows what. We must interpret everything with judgment, thought, and discernment[16] blessed by God and see the Scriptures with spiritual eyes and glasses. Then God's Word will become clear and unified to us. For the great wars, victories, possessions and physical blessings in the law are now past and replaced in the Spirit. Therefore the prophet Joel, who was quoted, spoke of his contemporary Jewish era, after which, however, another time was to come, the era of which Isaiah, Micah, and others speak, when weapon shall not be lifted against weapon and there will henceforth be no more war, but they will put away their weapons, break them in pieces and burn them (Isa. 2:4; Mic. 4:3; Ps. 46:9; 76:4; Ezek. 39:9; Hos. 2:18). That is the kingdom of Christ, the time of Christians and our time, when it is no longer right for us to make or use such murderous weapons.

87 *Finally, there may be people so ungodly as to raise the objection that the prophet says and it is written, "Cursed be he who does the work of the Lord with slackness; and cursed be he who keeps back his sword from bloodshed" (Jer. 48:10).*

ANSWER: If one wanted to understand and use the Scripture in such an absurd way, those men would be the best who constantly shed blood. Far be it from a Christian to have such ungodly thoughts. The prophet is speaking here of the punishment of the sinful nation of the Moabites, whom God wanted to punish and devastate (Judg. 3:28). And in order to make the punishment so much more severe he encourages the avenger, whom he is sending, to carry it out without qualms. Therefore it is just the same as if the false prophets, or the world, who quote this passage were to say "Cursed be the Turk if he is indolent and negligent in punishing us and keeping back his sword from shedding our blood." Therefore, O woe to the blindness of this world, which tries to cover one blindness with another.

FURTHER CONSIDERATIONS

88 SINCE THE FATHERS AT FIRST also held that Christians may not go to war or serve as secular judges and that those in office were not regarded as Christians, let us look at some documents and testimonies that speak against their own practice.

Papal law specifies[17] that it is not fitting to kill anyone. Their code puts no one to death, but places excommunication on the wicked. The reason why these are not to be so punished is given in their decree, that those who are foreordained to salvation may better their lives. But the others will be damned, with all punishment deemed useless, referring to the example in Luke 9:51–56. Furthermore, those who take the sword shall be judged by the sword (IV. *Quidam; cum quisque; obtineri; ipsa pietas, Augusti*).

Thus, causa 23, questi 4, c. si ecclesia, also says that the true church persecutes no one but only suffers persecution, referring to the example of Sarah and Hagar, and others.

Chrysostom (who lived in 390) is strongly opposed to warfare and taking revenge because they have committed themselves to him who taught peace. Read his exposition of Matthew and John.

The Council of Elvira decided that magistrates should not be admitted into the church during the year that they serve. Indeed, many other decrees and many ancient teachers are opposed to the participation in war of those who are spiritual (which simply means the true Christians). [Note: they do not consider the worldly rulers to be Christians.][18]

In the Council of Toledo, held in Spain in the thirteenth year after the regulation, at the time of Honorius and Arcady, it was decided that whoever is a soldier after baptism shall never become a deacon even if he has not committed any specific deed in war.

In Canon 23, q.v., Circumcel.; pena illorum (punishment of those), it is more clearly stated by Augustine that heretics should not be punished by death. Chrysostom, discussing Matthew 13 on the tares, shares that view. The best ancient canons are also against this wantonness; they say that those who are spiritual should neither kill nor attack anyone for any reason at all (not to mention for the sake of one's faith). They should not do so themselves, nor delegate others, nor assist by word or deed, but also censure it in others (c. 23., quest. vlt. Chap).

It continued to be held until the time of Pope Pelagius, AD 553, that heretics should not be condemned to death nor should worldly authority be called on for assistance. He was the first to order that when a man refused to be persuaded by reasonable arguments, he should be forced and compelled to do so. This was done, and increased constantly with the passage of time.

Luther, in his sermon on Matthew 13:24–30, in the collection of sermons for home use, also speaks of the tares:[19] The church or the office of preaching does not wield the sword, but whatever it does it does solely with the Word. Therefore, he says, the ancient teachers are right in this matter. If Matthew, when he was still a tax collector, and Paul, when he was persecuting the Christians, and the thief on the cross had been sentenced and executed as wicked men (which they were) immediately after the deed, then the wheat which grew from them afterward (since they were won over) would have been uprooted.

But this is not to say that the church is to put the wicked to death with the sword. It is to ban and exclude them as heathen, so that they recognize their sin and mend their ways, and that others may be warned by their example and be watchful. [Just listen, you Lutherans, how well you follow him!][20] Do you say, Why does one not deal thus with thieves, murderers and others, for some might be saved and repent?

ANSWER: Here you must understand that the Lord is speaking of the kingdom of Christ. That is where no sword is to used, lest the wheat be torn out with the tares. [That is what Luther says; however, when we say it, we are called heretics.][21] But in the kingdom of the world God has given a different commandment, which is: "He who takes the sword shall perish by the sword" (Matt. 26:52).

Christ does not say a word here about that worldly realm. Therefore, they dare not be mixed together, but what applies to Christ's kingdom is supposed to be achieved there; then again, what applies to the realm of the world is supposed to be achieved there. This Luther himself says and writes.

89 PAUL THE APOSTLE WRITES to the believers, "Let the peace of Christ rule in your hearts, to this indeed you are called in one body" (Col. 3:15) (note that we are called to peace, and the one body is the Christian church). It is unfitting for a body to have a sword and use it against itself. It is a desperate act to commit suicide or injure oneself. It is gross foolishness if the body deliberately tried to injure its own members with the power of the sword. Thus it is completely inappropriate for the church of Christ to use the sword within itself. For they are all one body and members of one another (Rom. 12:5; 1 Cor. 12:12; Eph. 1:23; 4:4; 5:1–14; Col. 1:17; 2:19).

Therefore, a person who is a servant of the worldly sword demonstrates clearly that he is not a member of the true Christian church. For no member holds a sword over another. Would it not be absurd if both hands of one body each had a sword and stabbed and struck each other and became disunited from one another? That is how it is if you say that Christians can be soldiers and use the sword. Therefore a ruler cannot be a Christian. It is not we who say this but Christ and his apostles, if one considers and studies their words.

90 PETER THE APOSTLE SAYS, "To this you have been called, because Christ also suffered for us, leaving us an example, that we should follow in his steps. He committed no sin; no guile was found on his lips. When he was reviled, he did not revile in return; when he suffered, he did not threaten; but he trusted to him who judges justly" (1 Pet. 2:21–23). See, that is the road on which Christians must also walk. They must suffer here without reviling when reviled, or threatening when they suffer, but commit everything to God, the just Judge (1 Pet. 3:9; Ps. 7:2 ff)."For the Lord is an avenger in all these things" (1 Thess. 4:6). How could they then use the power of the sword, if he is to be Judge and Avenger? Absolutely not!

91 WHEN DAVID HAD THE ARK of God brought out of the house of Abinadab into the house of Obededom, and the oxen stumbled and Uzzah put his hand on the ark of God and held it, "the anger of the Lord was kindled against Uzzah, and God smote him there" because of his wicked deed, and he died there by the ark (2 Sam. 6:1 ff). This shows and represents figuratively that God neither wants nor needs men to defend, fight for, or preserve the gospel with a human arm or the power of the sword, as though he were a god like an idol, unable to defend his Word and gospel himself.

92 "IF A MAN IS BURDENED with the blood of another, let him be a fugitive until death; let no one help him," said Solomon (Prov. 28:17). Hence, a Christian cannot with good conscience help toward shedding blood, much less participate in it himself. God says through Isaiah, "Even though you make many prayers, I will not listen; your hands are full of blood," "and your fingers with iniquity" (Isa. 1:15 and 59:3). Therefore a Christian cannot stain and spot himself with blood; for the soul is in the blood (Gen. 9:4), and blood is surely not water.

93 CHRIST SAYS TO HIS FOLLOWERS, "Whatever you wish that men would do to you, do so to them; for this is the law and the prophets" (Matt. 7:12; Luke 6:31; Sir. 31:15; Tob. 4:16). That is how it is to be in the true Christian church. But nobody who is Christian likes to have a sword used against him. Hence, no Christian should do so to another. Nobody wants to be tortured, bloodily attacked or killed; hence he should not do so to another. Nobody likes to be oppressed by reviling, quarreling, violence and injustice; therefore let him not do so to his neighbor. Nobody likes to be hit, given blows, or to be harmed in any other way, even if this is done by someone who has forgotten his Christian honor; since he does not like it, he should not do it to others. Otherwise each would be like all the others, guilty of the law and the prophets, even of natural law. And this removes the sword, force and worldly authority from the Christian church.

On the contrary, among the worldly Christians who still do to others what they themselves do not like and who by no means love their neighbor as themselves, there the sword and force are necessarily decreed. But among those who love, it is not given. Those who do not steal have no need of a hangman among them – much less, that they themselves be executioners. In the same way, Christians who do to others what they themselves like to receive and who love one another as themselves have no need of a government with the sword in their midst or among them to compel them to do good or to prevent their doing evil.

But in the world government is more necessary and essential than a bridle for a horse if people are to be controlled. But wherever anyone in the church of Christ ignores this law, "Love your neighbor as yourself" (Matt. 22:39) or conversely, "what you do not want done to you, don't do to your neighbor," and if he demonstrates disloyalty and wrong or evil, and does not accept being admonished or disciplined through the discipline and punishment of the Spirit or even through the Word of the Lord, he is no Christian and it is Christ's command to put him out of the church by means of the ban. Then he is part of the world under the sword and must submit to the law until he returns through repentance and a mending of life (Gal. 3).

If the church of Christ were to have the sword, it would have no need of the ban or exclusion and Christ would not have said, "If he refuses to listen to the church, let him be to you as a heathen and a tax collector" (Matt. 18:17).

94 CHRIST IS A KING of peace, foreshadowed by Solomon and Melchizedek, who was king of Salem, that is, of peace (Heb. 7:2). Therefore also in the Christian church, indeed, in the house of Christ, peace is mayor, the bailiff and steward, not the sword (Isa. 60:17); there will be a great peace there (2 Esd. 13:12). True Christians are a peaceful people of which the prophets foretold (Ps. 72:7). For David also says, "May the Lord bless his people with peace" (Ps. 29:11). "He who would love life, . . . let him seek peace and pursue it" (Ps. 34:12, 14; 1 Pet. 3:11; 2 Tim. 2:22)."Great peace will they have who love your law" (Ps. 119:165). "Peace be within your walls" (Ps. 122:7). "Peace be upon Israel!" (Ps. 125:5; Gal. 6:16). And Isaiah: "You, Creator, will bring about peace, for we trust in you" (Isa. 26:3). And "my people shall dwell in the tents of peace" (Isa. 32:18). Also: "They shall live and move in peace; my servants will rejoice from their hearts" (Isa. 55:12; 65). "I will let peace flow to her like rivers of water" (Isa. 66:12). "For the fear of God," says Sirach, "is a crown of wisdom and makes peace flourish again" (Sir. 1:11). Yes, Christ commands his followers to say when they enter a house, "Peace be to this house. And if a son of peace is there, your peace shall rest upon him; but if not, it shall return to you" (Matt. 10:12–13; Luke 10:5–6).

Thus, Christians are children of peace. "Peace I leave with you," says Christ, "my peace I give to you; not as the world gives give I to you" (John 14:27). After his resurrection, when all the doors were closed Jesus came and stood among them and said to his disciples, "Peace be with you" (John 20:19). That word is the first that Jesus spoke after his resurrection; then, showing them his hands and his side, he said again, "Peace be with you."

All the Lord's apostles first of all and always wish true peace to the churches, which is the apostolic and Christian greeting (Rom. 1:7; 1 Cor. 1:3; 2 Cor. 1:2; 1 Pet. 1:2; 2 Pet. 1:2; 2 John 1:3; Jude 1:2; Rev. 1:4)."For God is not a God of confusion but of peace," says Paul (1 Cor. 14:33). In all the congregations of the saints, may "peace be with all of you" (Rom. 15:33). "Agree with one another, live in peace, and the God of love and peace will be with you" (Phil. 4:9; 2 Cor. 13:11). And we should wear the shoes of peace (Eph. 6:15). Also: "Strive for peace with all men" (Heb. 12:14). "For," says James, "where jealousy and selfish ambition exist, there will be disorder and every vile practice.... And the harvest of righteousness is sown in peace by those who make peace" (James 3:16, 18).

In the church of Christ, then, where such peace exists, there is no sword or rulership, nor should there be. But in the world, where such peace does not exist, there the sword is and must be. Although God has offered his peace to all mankind, they have not all accepted it; therefore, lest worse happen to men, God in his grace has instituted authority on earth and rulers in the world so that (especially for the sake of the good) outward peace may be kept, which must by no means be taken to mean the true, inward peace of God, which cannot exist together with private possessions. For the world observes peace only for the sake of its possessions; if it is offended in that regard, peace is at once lost. They therefore do not have the peace that Christ has given to his people.

95 AMONG THOSE in whose life Christ and his teaching truly reign, all carnal rulership is at an end. And among those over whom physical, carnal rulership reigns, Christ is at an end. He has to leave the country of the Gadarenes for he never ever will protect their self-interest, nor does he spare their hogs when those who were possessed are freed (Matt. 8:34).

96 THE SUPREME LORD, Christ himself, did not come to reign, conquer, pass judgment, or rule, nor have anybody brought before him for judgment (John 5:45), nor did he himself want to bring charges against anyone; on the contrary, he himself served, and let himself be ruled, attacked, sentenced and condemned to death, and to accept injustice; in brief he suffered. That is our mirror into which we want to look, in which we want to see whether we have the form of Christ or not. Then the dissension over government would soon be eliminated.

97 CHRIST SAID, "Whoever would save his life will lose it" (Matt. 16:25). Therefore, whoever tries to protect and defend his earthly life and whatever else he has, will squander and forfeit life eternally in God's sight; and whoever loses his life will keep it for eternal life. Only a slight defense is required: it is simply turning around and presenting oneself at the foot of the cross of Christ. That is the defense of Christians, in which they will overcome and receive victory (Rom. 8:37) for eternal life (not for earthly life). For earthly victory does not bring about permanent victory, for there is always a stronger power that will in turn conquer and rule over the Christian. This is therefore not the victory of Christ but the victory of reprehensible flesh that will perish with the flesh.

98 PAUL SAYS, "As servants of God we commend ourselves in every way: through great endurance, in afflictions, hardships, calamities, beatings, imprisonments, riots, labors, sleepless nights, hunger; by purity, knowledge, patience, kindness, holiness of spirit, genuine love, truthful speech, and the power of God; with the weapons of righteousness for the right hand and for the left; in honor and dishonor, in ill repute and good repute. We are treated as impostors, and yet are true; as unknown, and yet are well-known; as dying, and see – we are alive; as punished, and yet not killed; as sorrowful, yet always rejoicing; as poor, yet making many rich; as having nothing, and yet possessing everything" (2 Cor. 6:4–10).

This is the promise and expectation of God's servants here on earth. Neither to the right nor to the left do they have anything but the weapons of righteousness, which are not swords, spears or other arms for taking life, but those weapons named at length above – especially great patience, which is a weapon for all conflict. Anyone who seeks Christ anywhere but at the foot of the cross in patience will not find him. He who teaches otherwise shows himself to be an Antichrist, liar and seducer.

99 IN THE FIRST apostolic conference it was decided that they keep themselves from blood, as they then wrote to the church: "It has seemed good to the Holy Spirit and to us to lay upon you no greater burden than these necessary things: that you abstain from what has been sacrificed to idols, from blood, from what is strangled, and from unchastity" (Acts 15:28–29). Here he stresses abstention from blood. For the Holy Spirit does not mean this in the sense of the prohibition of the law of Moses (but as the Psalmist also said: "Their drink offerings of blood I will not pour out" (Ps. 16:4), rather, it was revealed only for this end time. As soon as worldly power mixed itself into the kingdom of Christ, the eating of blood – that is, shedding the blood of man – began among supposed Christians, which the Holy Spirit now correctly forbids us to do as the children of God, whereby we need to be vigilant. If we do so, we do what is right.

100 PAUL SAYS, "EVEN IF WE, or an angel from heaven, should preach to you a gospel contrary to that which we have preached to you, let him be accursed. As we have said before, so now I say again, If anyone is preaching to you a gospel contrary to that which you have received, let him be accursed" (Gal. 1:8–9). If the priests and teachers of war are by no means angels, and preach another gospel that brings with it the sword, guns, spears, armor, lances, clubs, executioners, bailiffs, fighting-masters, tower confinement, imprisonments, warfare, bloodshed, murder, beating and anger, which we have not received from the apostles, they are therefore accursed together with their teaching.

101 GOD DID NOT GIVE the tribe of Levi any part of the land in the promised land (Deut. 18:2; Num. 18:20; Ezek. 44:48), nor command or permit them to be earthly rulers. This figuratively represents our priesthood in Christ and was descriptive of us, as Paul writes to the Hebrews (Heb. 7:5, 8, 9, 10). Christ himself says, "The Son of man has nowhere to lay his head" (Luke 9:58), that is, he had no possessions or ruling position here on earth. If he did not have these things, much less should we, his disciples.

102 THE WORLD and false Christians boast of their love for their neighbor, saying: Should I not come to the rescue of my neighbor who is threatened with death and I can prevent it? This is the obligation of everyone, God has commanded it; for what I like to have done for me I should also do for others. Answer: This kind of physical aid is what Peter wanted to give the Lord (Matt. 26:51). But hear what Christ did: The Lord restored health to the one whom Peter struck and injured out of physical love for Christ – so strongly did the Lord reject any help or love by which others might be harmed or hated, as he still does today. Yes, we are to love only, and not to hate our worst enemies (Luke 6:35), even if they injure us collectively or individually. "If one member suffers, all suffer together," says Paul (1 Cor. 12:26).

Out of Christ's love come forbearance and love, hence we are not to injure anyone out of love for another; otherwise we abandon love for our enemies and miss the way of Christ, and only an outward alliance of mutual help as practiced in the whole world would result: If you help me, I will help you. But wherever true Christians can come to the aid of others in distress, be they friend or foe, if it can be given without injury to anyone, there it will never cease or be lacking among believers and followers of Christ because true Christian love injures nobody, neither friend nor foe.

103 PEOPLE MAY ALSO SAY: It cannot be proved by any Scripture that one should not carry a sword. In reply, one should know that it is made abundantly clear in many ways in Scripture that revenge, war, anger, and force are forbidden. If those things are forbidden, then the weapons used for them are also forbidden. For if you are ordered to stop keeping hogs in order to become a town councilor, you will also be ordered to lay aside the cudgel used for the hogs. You want to be a Christian, but hypocritically carry the sword or other weapon to pretend you are not a Christian; you want to be a disciple of Christ, yet at the same time want to be seen as conforming to the world. But such two-faced, double-minded hypocrites, like mules – neither horse nor real donkey – who still want to please the world and hide behind its shield as brothers, are not servants of Christ but servants and slaves of the world to which they want to conform (Gal. 1:10).

104 THEY ARE QUICK TO ACCUSE US, as the Jews did Christ and his followers: They want to oppose the emperor, forbid interest-taking, be disobedient, have no government, be lords themselves and call themselves King of the Jews and the like. But in their intoxication and with overflowing malice, they are really accusing Christ and his followers, who are innocent and have put away the sword and ruling power and are sheep ready for slaughter. But let one of the children of the world and of all the supposed Christians, new and old,[22] who want to keep the worldly sword, emerge as contender, then see whether they do not quarrel about earthly rulership and seek to dominate physically with their mercenaries. Would to God it were not so that each wants to rule in order that no one may lord it over him!

As for us, we simply remain servants like our Master and Christ, who came not to be served (Matt. 10:45 and elsewhere); we cannot be concerned with worldly authority. We need not worry about governments; there are enough rulers to be found. Let us simply see to it that we remain Christians, endure, and win the victory of the Lamb to the glory of the Father and Christ.

105 PAUL THE APOSTLE SAYS, "It is no longer I that live but Christ who lives in me" (Gal. 2:20) and "Christ is my life" (Phil. 1:20) – in whom Christ, and not he himself, lives. Even if a person were also a ruler, Christ would indeed verify in him exactly that which Christ himself did, namely, that his kingdom is not of this world

(John 18:36), from which he fled when he was about to be made king and a high ruler (John 6:15), that he refused to judge in the division of the inheritance (Luke 12:14), and that he refused to pass the death sentence on the woman taken in adultery (John 8:11). In every believer in whom Christ lives he still does not do such things.

106 CHRIST COMMANDS THAT forgiveness of sins in his name be proclaimed to the whole world (Luke 24:47), and in our Christian faith we confess and say: one holy Christian church, in which there is forgiveness of sins. All of this would be futile, yes, the preaching of repentance would be useless, if we Christians were to pass a death sentence, because sinners would thereby be deprived of this grace. Therefore, judgment over life and limb is not the business of the Christian. If it is our duty to forgive sinners their sins and transgressions for the sake of the name of Jesus Christ, the just judge, how can we then condemn sinners to death? Christ's words would also be futile when he told Peter how often to forgive his brother (Matt. 18:–22). For if we were to keep the law of Moses according to the letter, nothing could be forgiven the offender. For as soon as the sinner's sin is revealed, the verdict of the law would also have to be pronounced on him.

107 THE WORLD HAS ITS LAWS; the Jews or the people of Moses had in their time their special system of laws over life and limb, far different from the world's system. Christians and their gospel also have their special system of laws and order given by Christ their King, not in accord with the Jewish law. For the kingdom of Christ is not physical but spiritual; it is a kingdom of peace and of the spiritual Melchizedek, where there is no strife nor lawsuit, nor use of the sword. Therefore the one must not be mixed with the other – the sword of the world put together with Moses and Christ, as the supposed Christians do. It is as harmonious as considering turnip greens and peas to be one and the same thing. O blindness and confusion! – Amen.

NOTES

1. See Robert Friedmann, "Article Book, Hutterite," *Mennonite Encyclopedia* 1, 173–4; Leonard Gross, *The Golden Years of the Hutterites* (Kitchener, Ontario: Pandora Press, [Revised Ed.] 1998), 210–15.

2. The Swiss Brethren, too, created a composite, book-length manuscript broadly circulated in 1575 entitled (in English translation): "A short, simple discourse on the thirteen articles which were debated in 1571 at Frankenthal in the Palatinate, composed for all those to consider and pass judgment on, who, beloved by God, desire the truth and want to be without human bias; also written as a justifiable warning, founded upon God's Word, to all magistrates who claim for themselves the gospel and the name Christian, yet who attempt at the same time through coercion to force and compel people against their wills into faith." *Mennonite Quarterly Review,* January 2000.

3. "[Vierter Artikel], [Vom Schweerdt], Das die Christen nit mögen krüegen, noch das weltlich Gericht und Schweerdt oder Gwalt füeren, und die in solchem Ambt nit für Christen gehalten können werden," (*Glaubenszeugnisse oberdeutscher Taufgesinnter II*, ed., Robert Friedmann [Heidelberg: Gütersloher Verlagshaus Gerd Mohn, 1967]), 239–298.

4. Reference to the Peace of Augsburg, 1555.

5. "and my son will not rule over you" was omitted in Friedmann, 1967, but is in codex EAH 227.

6. This is the theme of the so-called theology of martyrdom of the Anabaptists, expecting and accepting suffering and persecution as something unavoidable in this world. The Anabaptists found the biblical foundation for this already in the Book of Daniel. See Robert Friedmann, "Martyrdom, Theology of," *Mennonite Encyclopedia* III, 519–21.

7. 2 Esd 2:26. This book is missing in all Protestant Bibles, but is found at the end of the complete Latin Vulgate. It has to do with a late-Jewish apocalypse, around A.D. 100. The book is usually included as one of the Jewish pseudo-epigraphs, strongly influenced by the (Pharisaic) Schamai school. Chapters 3 to 14 are original; chapters 1, 2 and 15, 16 are later Christian additions. The Anabaptists Michael Sattler and Peter Riedemann quote from this book. See Robert Friedmann, "Ezra, IV," *Mennonite Encyclopedia* II, p 283 f.

8. This paragraph is a clear reference to the practice of *cuius regio eius religio:* where one resides decides one's religion, and within that region no other religion can be tolerated – a principle proposed at the Diet of Speyer in 1526 and confirmed in the Peace of Augsburg in 1555.

9. The phrase, "but in the world the sword has precedence" is missing in Friedmann, but found in Codex EAH 227.

10. Friedmann, 1967, p. 269, reads: "in seiner handt." However, Cod. EAH 227 reads: "in seinem mundt," which fits better into the context.

11. Reference to the Jewish war. The Book of Josephus Flavius was popular among the Anabaptists.

12. In Friedmann, the text reads: "freundtschafft" whereas codex EAH 227 reads: "feündtschafft."

13. "nit du, sonder ir."

14. This passage from Luke was unfortunately cited, again and again, in order to justify coercive conversion into the established church

(especially through the Inquisition). This interpretation dates back to Augustine.

15. Translated directly from the Froschauer Bible. NRSV reads: "But I have not run away from being a shepherd in your service, nor have I desired the fatal day. You know what came from my lips." See also Ezek. 18:23, 32; 33:11.

16. "Wir müessen mit einem gotsälligen urtaill eintruckh und gespaltnen klauen alle dinge verstehen . . .": the original, "gespaltnen klauen" (cloven hoofs – see Lev 11:3), is translated here, "discernment." This image was used by other Anabaptists as well; see Van der Zijp, "Gespauwde Klauw," *Mennonite Encyclopedia* II, p. 508.

17. All references in this point, except for the citation from Luther, come from Sebastian Franck, *Geschychtbibel,* mostly from pp. 388r ff.

18. In the margin.

19. Taken from the edition of *Veit Dietrich*, first published in 1544 (Weimar Edition 52, 134, 7 ff), discussed by Roland H. Bainton: "Religious Liberty and the Parables of the Tare" (Bainton: *Early and Medieval Christianity,* Boston, 1962, 112 f).

20. In the margin.

21. In the margin.

22. Probably Protestant and Catholic.

RELATED PLOUGH TITLES

Bearing Witness
Edited by Charles E. Moore and Timothy Keiderling
Stories of Christian martyrs from around the world and through the ages to inspire and challenge the next generation of believers.

Brotherly Community
The Highest Command of Love
Andreas Ehrenpreis, Claus Felbinger
These two early Anabaptist documents, from 1560 and 1650, give an impassioned witness to the life of discipleship of Jesus and to the possibility of true brotherly love in full community.

Love Is Like Fire
The Confession of an Anabaptist Prisoner
Peter Riedemann
A spirited confession of faith by a twenty-three-year-old persecuted Christian in a sixteenth-century Austrian dungeon.

Plough Publishing House
1-800-521-8011 ◆ 845-572-3455

PO BOX 398 ◆ Walden, NY 12586 ◆ USA
Brightling Rd ◆ Robertsbridge ◆ East Sussex TN32 5DR ◆ UK
4188 Gwydir Highway ◆ Elsmore, NSW 2360 ◆ Australia

www.plough.com